p.53 + — 108 —
p 106 — 108 — on leadership
A Church out of touch.
p.121 – 123 + His conclusion re this
p.132 what Willie Walsh & Donal Murray: Bishops say about what is needed
pp 150–151 –
p 225 – Late Cardinal Carlo Martini on the State of the Church today;
+ p 229 Timothy Radcliffe
pp 136/137 Cult of priesthood

Harry Bohan

NB

SWIMMING UPSTREAM

Finding Positives in a Negative Ireland

p. 237 Willie Walsh – Bishop

the columba press

First published in 2013 by
the columba press
55A Spruce Avenue, Stillorgan Industrial Park,
Blackrock, Co. Dublin

Cover by sin é design
Origination by The Columba Press
Printed by Bell & Bain Ltd

ISBN 978 1 85607 802 3

All royalties from the sale of this book will be donated to the Cahercalla Community Hospital & Hospice, Ennis, Co. Clare

TABLE OF CONTENTS

ACKNOWLEDGEMENTS

The writing of a book is made possible by the encouragement of others. It would not be easy to mention all their names here but there are a few people I need to thank. Over the past couple of years Willie Walsh has been encouraging priests from within our diocese of Killaloe to write their story and he was certainly the main reason why I agreed to put pen to paper. I owe a great debt to John Quinn for all his help. He accompanied me in the early stages of the journey and helped to give this book structure and direction.

Maureen Kelly, Annette Shanahan and Irene Fleming played a big part in clarifying and giving meaning to some of the ideas, issues and initiatives.

A special word of thanks to Marguerita McNamara and Puff O'Connor for the many hours they spent typing and for their patience with me.

The final outcome of the book is, however, my own responsibility, flaws and all.

Lastly I wish to record my thanks to the publishers, Columba Press, and particularly to Michael Brennan who played a huge role in getting me to put pen to paper.

Foreword

I am happy and privileged to write a foreword of welcome to the publication of *Swimming Upstream* by Fr Harry Bohan who has been a colleague and friend of mine for many years. I believe that this is a rather special book because it is one man's unique vision of Church that is both rooted in and the fruit of over fifty years of priesthood. His was and is a priesthood that was never lived at an academic remove but is a priesthood of action and involvement. 'Swimming upstream' aptly sums up the man who was never content to go with the flow but always prepared to explore differing directions and possibilities, even if this involved his having to adopt positions that went against the current of popular or accepted norms.

This book reveals that Harry Bohan the man and the priest are synonymous. It discloses modestly and without fanfare a lifetime of involvement and achievement. It hardly needs saying that all of his life's vision was directed towards and enacted within the setting of parish life. His life's work was parochial in the best sense of the words which are 'community building'. The range of initiatives which he has been involved in is impressive to say the least: rural housing, the Céifin project, urban development, rural resources, the establishment of a community hospital, the reopening of a cattle mart, the GAA and various other cultural activities. All of these were community-enriching activities that he saw as part and parcel of his normal priestly ministry of the Sacraments and Preaching God's Word.

Swimming Upstream presents Harry Bohan's vision of Church as one where priest and people are united in their engagement with the practical issues of daily life. It seems to grow out of a natural awareness that where people are there is God and there too is God's servant – the priest. On the one hand it seems a traditional view of Christian life but on reflection it is a radical partnership born out of the vision of the Second Vatican Council. Fr Harry Bohan launched his vision on the very first tide of the Council's renewal and today he remains as committed to a love of his Church, its people and his priesthood as he was fifty years ago.

Over the past two years Fr Harry has experienced a serious illness which he has borne with much dignity and without complaint. I feel this book is a positive sign of his welcome recovery. Forgive me if I linger a moment longer on his illness but I am struck by something Harry himself has written about it in this book: It is 2012 and he is back home after a stay in hospital, the fifth in eighteen months. He is in physical pain one night and with that comes the often accompanying unrest of thinking. Being Harry the thinking is about the challenges facing the

Church and one can almost feel his physical pain mirroring a mental anguish for the state of the Church.

Being Harry also means that his sense of spirituality is never far away and so his thoughts move into a *de profundis*-like state as he wonders to himself: 'Where is John (O'Donohue) now when we need him to help us identify the riches that emerged from our Celtic past?' There is something poetic and saving in Harry's response to this question and he writes in a very tender way: 'I lay back in my bed and tried to enter that world, seeking healing for my own wounds.'

It bears all the marks of the man who sees God in the hospital, at the sickbed, the conference hall, the sanctuary, the sports field, the cattle mart, the community hall and the parishioner's house. It should be of little wonder to us that in his own hour of pain he doesn't complain but seeks out and easily finds God in the monastery of his own mind.

I salute the man and his fine book which gives insight into our present time, a reminder of fields we have furrowed and a beacon of hope for the future.

Willie Walsh

A Great Friend and Confidant

My first memories of Fr Harry Bohan date back to when I was a small lad. Coming from a family steeped in Clare and Clarecastle hurling, the Clare team he brought to win two National League titles were certainly my childhood heroes. After Clare matches, I just couldn't wait to get home (if we ever got past Ryan's pub in Newport) to my hurley. Hour after hour was spent in the garden, until my mother would call me in from the dark. I would become Jackie O' Gorman, Sean Stack or our own local hero John Callinan. I can safely say that it was Harry's team that instilled a dream in me to some day win that Munster title!

Although always aware of Harry, I first got to hear him speak publicly in 1984 at a Mass in our local church. I can honestly say that the man made a definite impact on this fifteen-year-old. I could tell that Fr Harry was a man of strong conviction. He always emphasised the importance of nurturing and cherishing a sense of community. My everlasting impression was how from the altar he described us as 'not a club at all, but a tribe'. Again I ran home to get out the hurley!

Harry and I would not have crossed paths too often over the next decade except when I would meet him after the great Clare victories of the 1990s. We often chatted late into the night, over a pint or two, on how we had made our great breakthrough. He was so relieved that the famine had ended.

So that was the story of 'the priest and I' until out of the blue in late 2003 the Clare County Board approached me to take over as hurling manager for two to three seasons. I was a greenhorn at that level back then but I immediately secured the services of one of the best coaches I've ever come across in Wolfe Tones' Alan Cunningham. I decided I needed a bit of experience in my corner so I rang Harry and asked him to meet me for a cup of tea. He was convinced I just wanted a bit of advice and was fairly gobsmacked when I told him he was a selector … end of story!

The rest is history. We won no major titles but we had a great squad that gave us everything. We were beaten by a last-gasp Cork point in the All-Ireland semi-final in 2005, I think we were never as low as after that defeat.

Harry was more than just a selector to the players. No, Harry was like a modern-day sports psychologist. He'd meet lads for breakfast, lunch and dinner to discuss mostly personal issues – I never interfered too much. Every one of the guys on that 2004/2006 squad valued Fr Harry's contribution and during that time he treated them all as family.

I've stayed in regular contact with Harry and he has become a great friend and confidant. He strongly believes in all things *local* being absolutely crucial in a world gone mad with technology. He would see more value in a twenty-minute visit to an elderly neighbour than any events which the world around was getting caught up in. 'That's real community,' he'd say.

A truly great human being who I'm privileged to say is my friend.

Anthony Daly

Introduction

In the spring of 2012, I was approached by Michael Brennan of Columba Press who suggested I should write a book of my experiences as a priest and the initiatives I had an involvement in down through the years. He had put a similar proposition to Bishop Willie Walsh who deftly directed him towards myself, commenting, 'Harry might not be around much longer,' a fair assessment as I was battling with cancer at the time. My response was that I was not interested in writing a memoir 'ego-trip' as there was an oversupply of those already. I agreed to write of the issues and the implemented initiatives that define me in a priesthood of fifty years, in the humble hope that they might appeal or even inform people somewhere, sometime.

I was born and raised in Feakle, Co. Clare, a strong self-reliant local community where emigration was a hard fact of life. Family and community shaped and formed me, emphasis on education and religion informed me in opting for the priesthood and I was ordained into the new Ireland of the 1960s. With some foresight my bishop, Joseph Rodgers, sent me to further my studies in the University of Wales in preparation for the new challenges of an industrialised society. He needed a priest who would understand and address the impact of rapid change and the needs of the diocese in responding to that change. In October 1963 I left a land of small farms, villages and towns, and, by European standards, two cities (Dublin and Cork) and returned to a very different Ireland in 1968. The centralisation of power and economic development both had a major impact on settlement patterns with the growth of housing estates and the consequent depopulation of villages and rural areas. A new model of Church was being laid down by the Vatican Council, one based on participation, the people of God, where everyone has a place. There was hope and it was a good time to be part of a new Ireland and a renewed Church.

In a sense this book is about reading the 'signs of the times'. It is about emphasising the importance of an engaged Christianity – one that doesn't turn its back on the world but engages with it. That is best lived in families and local communities. These two systems that held Irish society and its people together for generations are now being undermined. The sense of belonging and the bonds of neighbours are weakened. After decades of movement away from the local and towards the global, Ireland has bought into a system of people being disengaged from one another.

Today there is a deep and corrosive loneliness engrained in our society, once prized and praised for its friendliness, welcoming-nature and unlocked doors. It was a place where children roamed freely and safely and were fed at every table. This is the living memory of many who now feel detached, unconnected and confused. Mental health is suffering. Suicide rates are on the increase, especially among our young men.

Out of crisis comes opportunity which, now recognised, can be grasped and the direction for a new society order determined. Irish society is at a crossroads. Self-reliance and self-resilience need once again to be cultivated and encouraged. This book is about practical ways and initiatives which clearly indicate the power and effectiveness of a people who take responsibility for themselves and their future. It is clear to me that the community can respond to the challenges of balancing the local with the global. The pendulum swings back from the supreme pursuit of individual celebrity and gratification which defined the latter stages of the Celtic Tiger era in Ireland. It may not always be articulated but there are definite signs of a search for spiritual meaning and ethical values in business and trade. There's a search for simplicity, a withdrawal from the rat race. There is a desire by many for a more wholesome life with God at the core. This book seeks to highlight that in spite of the extraordinary changes in thinking, lifestyle, behaviour and belief, people are still in search of a supportive network of community where they can contribute and share their lives.

The need to reset the power base to the local community is now immediate. As a student, I read a book that greatly influenced my thinking called *Small is Beautiful: A Study of Economics as if People Matter* by E.F.

Schumacher. It summarised what Vatican II was about and embraced the reality of life for people in a changing world. This informed my thinking and was behind many of the initiatives described in this book.

I have lived through a time when institutions and big business disengaged from people, when people disengaged from one another. I have seen individuals, families and local communities feeling powerless in the face of banks, governments, churches and big companies which simply do not take account of people. This book is an effort to articulate a different vision and to work towards an alternative model which involves people taking back their own power. It is only then that people can take responsibility.

Jesus Christ established communities and engaged with the world through His presence among the people. He prayed, ate, fasted, healed, mourned and celebrated with the people. Our Church is called to live as He lived. I believe deeply in Christ and the Christian story. Nourishing the faith and finding ways to connect first to one's own life and then to the reality of the lives of other people we are called to serve can help us all 'to be that change'. Simply and humbly, this book is an effort to gather together the experiences and initiatives which have been part of my life, and to hold up a mirror to the reality of the changing Irish society that prevailed.

I hope you enjoy reading it and take something from it.

ONE

Remembering Mary Ryan

Mary Ryan died on the eve of St Patrick's Day, 2012, six weeks after she had celebrated her 100th birthday. She had married Dan Ryan in 1940 and settled in their farmhouse a few miles out from Sixmilebridge, Co. Clare. Mary Begley, her maiden name, had originally come from just a mile down the road, so all her long life was circumscribed in one small geographical area. Mary and Dan reared eleven children, one of whom tragically died in a car accident. As her parish priest in her latter years, I regularly ministered to Mary and brought her communion every month. In so doing I got to know her story. Her life, her outlook and her values impressed me greatly. She died in her own house and on the eve of her funeral I talked with her family in that house about how best we could remember Mary. Five strands to her life emerged:

Self-reliance

Mary worked hard all her life, inside and outside the house, as was the tradition. She lived through two world wars and an economic war, through rationing and emigration (although none of her own children emigrated). Despite the lean times she coped and provided for her large family who were always warm and well-fed. ('I remember her cutting *sciolláns* [seed-potatoes] in that corner,' a son remarked.)

Neighbours

Mary enjoyed the company of her neighbours at two levels – as regular night-time visitors who told stories and shared news at her fireside, and also as co-workers who helped at saving the hay, cutting the turf, etc. The concept of neighbourhood and community were crucial to her life.

Health

Mary would rarely have visited a doctor. In her time it would have taken something exceptional to cause her to see the doctor or go to hospital. Her family ate good, home-produced, nutritious food. Mary was producing *organic* food before the word was invented. Her household was largely self-sufficient.

Family

Mary lived for her family in providing food, clothing and – above all – love for them, although the word love might not have been used *per se*. It was a very caring environment – caring not just for family but for animals too. ('In that corner there, you might have a sick calf who needed special attention,' said Mary's son). It reminded me of a woman whom I used to visit many years ago in her thatched cottage near the airport. I was intrigued by the fact that the house seemed to have two front doors. 'Why was that?' I asked her. 'The other door was for the horse,' she replied. The horse was so vital to their lives that he was kept under the same roof.

Faith

Mary had an incredible belief in a God who was the power above and beyond herself and she submitted totally to His will. She would, of course, have absorbed that faith from her own parents, but she honed it in her own life in her reverence for the Eucharist, her devotion to the community gathering that was Sunday Mass and to the sacredness of the sacraments. She grew up in a Church that was very clerical and authoritarian, but a Church that was of its time. It was also a very devotional Church and Mary would always have found time for the sodality and the holy hour. She imparted a strong moral code to her children. She lived her faith.

It is obvious that all of this belongs to another, very different age and might be construed as a romantic, possibly idyllic view of a vanished Ireland, and when I reflected on Mary's life in this way at her funeral service, I certainly wasn't proposing turning the clock back fifty or sixty years. Even if we could, why would we want to?

What concerned me were those five *concepts* that underlined Mary Ryan's life – self-reliance, neighbours, health, family and faith. Maybe, after all the excesses of an economic boom and globalisation, we should reflect on whether we walked away too quickly from Mary Ryan's path and whether we should consider walking a while in her direction.

There is so much talk today of the need to rediscover neighbourliness and community. It was a crucial part of Mary Ryan's life but there is a dangerous isolation in today's housing estates. There is precious little contact or communication between 'neighbours', which seems totally contradictory to me. Someone said to me recently that a neighbour is someone who shares the same address as yourself – and that is it. That is very sad.

Again, everyone is screaming at the health services for their alleged inability to cope with severe pressure. I look once more to Mary Ryan who largely looked after her own health by eating the right food and availing of exercise through hard work. Maybe if we took small steps towards taking more responsibility for our own health, a lot of services could be freed up.

The family is under serious pressure also. One of the basic necessities for family life is proper housing. All through the boom times, housing was seen more as a commodity for trading. It was developer-driven and ultimately the burden of huge mortgages seriously damaged family life. Mary Ryan didn't have such a burden but she had the burden of caring for and providing for a large family in lean times – and she did so in a mainly self-sufficient way.

Above all, Mary put her trust in a provident God. The faith that she lived was bought at a massive price (I write this in Easter Week) which should remind us not to move too quickly away from it. We talk about the need for renewal in the Church today. The Second Vatican Council was all about renewal, when Pope John XXIII wanted to 'open the windows'. Unfortunately, in Ireland, we put most of the focus on liturgical renewal and paid too little attention to that great document, *The Church in the Modern World*. That is where our future lies.

Today many are turning to a contemplative way of life, seeking 'quiet times'. In many ways Mary Ryan had much of that in her otherwise busy life – in her holy hour, in her quiet praying time at home and in maintaining the sacredness of Sunday. Obviously we seek quiet and contemplation in different ways now, but the concept is the same. Those concepts that were part of Mary Ryan did not necessarily go out of date when Mary died. That is what I preached at her funeral service.

Roots that shaped me

Those five concepts – self-reliance, neighbours, family, health and faith – impacted greatly on my own life growing up in Feakle. Our home was an old-style pub which reached into nearly every room of the ground floor of the house. Growing up in a pub was interesting.

It is often said that it is the university of the people. They came, told their stories, often around the fire in the kitchen and shared their wisdom. My heroes – all local hurlers who had won five county championships – came into our pub, just as they came to the gathering at Sunday Mass. For me as a child, all of life was in Feakle. I remember telling my niece Áine once that when I was her age, if I got to Limerick I would be afraid of missing the bus home to Feakle.

I was the second child of four born to Michael and Bridget Bohan. My father was a garda who married into the pub, but the rule then was that he could not be posted to his homeplace. He spent most of his working life in Ennis. They were amazing parents who, like many of their generation, made serious sacrifices for their children's sake. He would cycle the eighteen miles out from Ennis of a summer morning (having been to Mass in the Friary) and cut or save turf (or do other seasonal work) all day, grab a few hours sleep and cycle back to Ennis for night duty. Such work paid for our education.

My mother was a strong and proud woman – a Women's Liberation advocate ahead of her time! She ran the pub and reared four children. She was very rooted in Feakle and had a great sense of place. My father was very capable and could have earned a promotion which would have meant moving to Co. Meath. Mother would not budge, however and so we stayed in Clare. Father retired early. At one stage, he had notions of buying a shop in Ennis, but again Mother was having none of it!

She passed that rootedness on to me. I still anxiously peruse the local paper to see if Feakle under-14s managed to beat Scariff!

The old saying 'It takes a village to rear a child' was never more true than in Feakle. The woman down the street was as likely to reprimand you for wrongdoing as your parents. Two doors from our pub lived Paddy and Nellie Loughnane who ran a shop, an undertaking business and a farm. They had no children of their own and from a very young age I spent a lot of time with them. I suppose they informally adopted me and I grew to love them and their world. Paddy loved dogs and horses and I developed a similar affection for those animals. They were beautiful people. There was much informal education in the way we watched and worked with our elders and acquired skills and much natural wisdom.

School was authoritarian, as was the fashion of the time, but it left no bad memories for me. What really impacted on me was the scourge of emigration with the consequent sundering of strong bonds of friendship which had been forged at school. Seven of the twelve of us who left school together emigrated, and all of us left the parish. Knowing the reality of emigration in my own village from an early age made a deep impression on me. Indeed, there is no doubt in my mind that some of the approaches and initiatives I would later get involved in were strongly influenced by knowing the pain of emigration at first-hand from an early age.

Community was very important in my youth. It was naturally present all about me – whether in the fireside discussions or in the Sunday gathering for Mass and the all-important after-Mass chats, and especially through our involvement with the GAA. We had our own local heroes who instilled in us a great pride in the parish as we strove to emulate their great deeds on the hurling pitch. Later when I boarded in St Flannan's College and in Maynooth seminary, I often wondered how I managed to spend twelve years separated from the people and the place that I loved so much.

As a family we were extremely conscious of our dependence on God. Faith permeated all aspects of our lives. Mass attendance was built into the structure of our lives. Prayer was important, necessary and habitual. Praying together was vital and the togetherness was as important as the prayer, although the image persists of saying the family rosary with beads in one hand and hurley in the other, hoping that the *trimmings* of the rosary would not have me late for hurling practice …

We rarely went to a doctor. We were born at home and cared for at home. Only once do I remember a doctor putting a bandage on me, when the shaft of a cart hit me in the ear. My father never complained of ill health but he collapsed and died in the church on Easter Sunday morning while the priest preached the Resurrection … From that day on, I was certain of an afterlife where we would be reunited.

I remember a conversation I once had with the playwright John B. Keane:

Me:	*Do you believe in heaven, John B?*
J.B:	*I do.*
Me:	*But people say no one ever came back to tell us …*
J.B:	*Didn't Himself come back and tell us there were many rooms in His Father's House? And if there isn't a heaven, where are your mother and father?*

So there are many ways in which my life has mirrored that of Mary Ryan. I feel we can still walk in Mary's footsteps. This is not an exercise in nostalgia nor an idealising of another era. We live amid great uncertainty. We don't know what the future will bring but we all need identity – to know who we are and how and where we fit into the scheme of things. I feel those Mary Ryan concepts will, in some different way, be crucial for our future. The Old Testament reminds us that there is nothing new under the sun. Things happen in different ways. We are all very brittle in the face of the total mystery of life. We are only here for a short time. All we can do is take more responsibility for our lives and put our trust in a greater power – and keep remembering Mary Ryan.

TWO

AWAY FROM HOME

I loved growing up in Feakle, so when the decision was made in 1952 to send me as a boarder to St Flannan's College, Ennis, it was a huge wrench for me. We lived eighteen miles from Ennis so a daily commute was out of the question and St Flannan's was the obvious choice for anyone in the Ennis hinterland who wanted secondary education. These were the years before free education. Education was very important to my parents' generation. They made enormous sacrifices to ensure that their children (four in our case) could have the opportunities they themselves did not have.

St Flannan's was also a junior diocesan college, so maybe the hope of a priest in the family was in my parents' heads, but it certainly wasn't in mine! And at the time, I hardly considered myself *fortunate* to be a boarder! It was heartbreaking to leave home each term and wonderful to come back.

It was not an easy time. Discipline was fairly heavy. I got into trouble for such *offences* as playing poker or smoking. A friend and I were reported for smoking in the toilets. We were given a serious lecture and six of the best with a cane. That didn't go down too well! Food was basic and scarce. I longed for the occasional parcel from home and often felt miserable on cold, wet evenings. Sport and study dominated our lives – and for me, sport meant hurling.

They say faith is caught, not taught. It is probably the same with vocations. I had no notion of a vocation in the early years in St Flannan's. Apart from occasional visits by recruiting missionary priests, there was no great encouragement towards the priesthood. What really inspired me, ultimately, was the example of two Feakle men, Kevin Hogan and Tim Tuohy, who were young priests when I was growing up. They were fine men who were greatly admired locally and who were very much of the community. Their witness impacted greatly on me. I talked it over with the college president and the then bishop, Joe Rodgers, a Killanena (just up the road from Feakle) man. The dye was cast. I would be going to Maynooth seminary.

Again, my decision demanded great sacrifices for my parents – fees, clothes, books, etc. They were a generation apart. We had the pub, a bit of a shop and my father's salary. On the face of it, not too bad, but there were four of us. They would also have to supplement these by cutting, saving and selling turf. We will never fully appreciate that generation. They were so loyal to each other, to family and to neighbours (especially to those who were in need). It is one of the reasons we can talk comfortably about them now.

How I became a priest I will never know. Having to leave the home and place to which I was so attached for another seven years was very difficult, and this time it meant leaving Clare too. I suppose my parents' sacrifice was an indication of serious purpose and, in a way, that helped me put up with the boarding.

Maynooth was a major culture shock. In terms of numbers, there were ninety of us first-years (four from my diocese) and as there were seven 'years' there would have been about five hundred students in all. There were six times more priests in Ireland in 1950 than in 1850, so the numbers in Maynooth in my time were an indication of the massive growth of a clerical Church. The students came from all over Ireland so the mix of accents was something new to me, although in effect a numbering system (I was number 12) meant that you stayed close to the same group all the way through college.

One of my closest friends was Joe Martin from Co. Tyrone. This was a whole new connection for me, to be meeting someone from over the border. Joe represented the Armagh diocese but was being ordained for the diocese of Seattle and was intended to go to Rome first to do a doctorate. On Ash Wednesday, a few months before ordination, Joe told me he was leaving Maynooth. This news came as a great shock to me. I was unsettled for some time after he left. He subsequently married and became head of an education board in Northern Ireland. He later wrote an excellent four-volume history of the GAA in Tyrone. We are still close friends. Many of my longest-lasting friendships were forged in Maynooth.

There were times when I thought of following Joe out the gate but I talked it over with the senior dean, Michael Harty (who would later become my bishop) and our spiritual advisor Jimmy Doherty. They both convinced me to stay. I suppose I interpreted this as a 'voice from above'! I also spoke a lot with Jimmy about the issue of celibacy. I had realised earlier that it was a massive sacrifice to make.

By and large, I would say the Church was blessed by the quality of the students of my time in Maynooth. Among them were some outstanding young men – both academically and on the sportsfields. I was middle-of-the-road in both. Sport kept a lot of us going. I have always maintained that the Maynooth senior football team of those years, for example, could have taken on and beaten the then All-Ireland champions. Hurling did not have the same numbers but we had a very competitive hurling league. The soccer teams represented dioceses – the Derry boys excelled here, whereas it's fair to say that Killaloe did not represent a threat! As captain of a hurling team, I asked Michael Harty for permission to invite a team from St Patrick's Training College to play us, but I was refused. It was a very enclosed environment.

Although we were seriously cut off from the world, I still enjoyed Maynooth. Facilities were basic enough. We read the newspapers in the billiard room. There was no radio or television. We had a shop for daily necessities. Everything happened within the walls. We held debates and staged plays. The Radio Éireann Symphony Orchestra recorded concerts in the *Aula Maxima* – we were considered an ideal audience! We studied in our rooms. I wonder now about the relevance of a lot of the stuff we studied, but we had to do it and we did it. It was only in later life, when I had experienced life, that I really appreciated philosophy and theology.

Among the staff a few people lifted life above the humdrum – Jimmy Doherty, Michael Harty, mentioned already, and Tomás Ó Fiach, later to become Cardinal and Archbishop of Armagh, for a start. The Professor of Sociology was Jeremiah Newman and of all the lectures in my time in Maynooth, his made the deepest impression on me, opening me to the changes that were happening in society. He invited guest speakers, including trade union leaders, to speak to us. This helped us to see that a largely rural Ireland was moving towards industrialisation and urbanisation. He instituted a study group in which we examined the great social encyclicals – *Rerum Novarum, Quadragesimo Anno, Mater et Magistra*. These documents had a lasting influence on me and would ultimately dictate the course of my priestly life.

And so, the seven years in Maynooth slipped by. One of my great fears in that time was that my parents would fall ill or die. I really loved the occasional visit they managed and it was heartbreaking to see them drive out the gate. Home, family and place were and would always be central to my life.

One of the great attractions of being home for the summer holidays from Maynooth was of course that I could resume hurling with my home club, Feakle. Meeting the lads I grew up with was as important as the hurling. We would often 'hang on' into the night after training for the chat. In 1958 we beat Whitegate in the first round of the Clare Championship and went on to meet Sixmilebridge in the semi-final. I was centre-field with my brother Mick. The match ended in a draw. It was a tough match – our Dermot Sheedy and their Mick Barron were sent off. It has been said to me that in Clare the passion at club level is much stronger than at county level …

The replay of that match was played at a ferocious intensity. I remember playing as if my life depended on it. I was marking Paddy Deasy … who ended up with a bandaged head! Later Michael Harty, my dean at Maynooth, who was at the match, commented to me, with a nod towards Deasy – 'That's why we don't like students playing club hurling.' Anyway, we won and faced St Joseph's in the final.

We trained for the final in the wettest three weeks you could imagine. Part of my fitness regime would be to run home from the fields or the bog where we were working. In the first of those weeks I developed pains, later diagnosed as a form of rheumatic fever. During the weeks leading up to the final, my father would light a fire during the night, at which I sat with blankets around my legs. On the morning of the final a former hurler, Bill Purcell, who was crippled at the age of twenty-eight called to our house. He heard I was going to play. 'If you play,' he said, 'you will finish up like me.'

The day of the final we met in the Queens Hotel. We walked to the field. Again because the weather was so bad, there was no pre-match parade. I should never have played. I stayed on until half-time and watched the second half in wet togs. We were beaten by seven points. Afterwards I went home instead of returning to the hotel. I spent the next eight months recovering. Thanks to my 'do-or-die' efforts, I was a regular attender at the infirmary in Maynooth.

THREE

LIFE IN THE CITIES

I was twenty-four years of age, going on twenty-five, when I was ordained a priest in Maynooth on 23 June 1963. I was one of sixty being ordained. Only the immediate family were allowed to attend, because of the numbers. It was a proud day for my parents, my family and for myself, as was the following day, when I celebrated my first Mass in Feakle. Us sixty young priests were witness to a transforming Ireland. In 1956 we had entered Maynooth from an old Ireland of economic stagnation and mass emigration. We emerged seven years later into a new Ireland of Lemass, industrial development, television, Vatican II, and later, free secondary education. This cumulation of events represented the most significant societal change in Ireland since the Famine. Our economy was opening to a wider world. The new 'job' world was the factory world.

On the day of my ordination, Joe Rodgers, the bishop of Killaloe, told me that on the advice of Jeremiah Newman, he was sending me to do postgraduate studies at the University of Wales in Cardiff. This was radically different to how I thought my life as a priest would be. I had anticipated being sent to a parish like Feakle and was initially disappointed at this news, but I had no say in the matter. Instead I was being asked to do further studies, not even in theology or a Church-related discipline. Later I would realise that in sensing the new Ireland, Joe Rodgers was ahead of his time. He realised that our diocese would be at the heart of radical change. Shannon with its airport, industrial estate, new town, and the Shannon development body would bring significant change to the whole of the mid-west region: Clare, Limerick, Tipperary North, all in our diocese. Bishop Rodgers told me that he was sending me to study so that the Church would have some understanding of this rapidly-changing world. A new road which I hadn't expected was opening up before me. I was taking my third major step away from home when I boarded an aeroplane for the first time on my way to a secular university in Cardiff.

I was to do a Master's degree on 'The Growth of Cities in Britain', under Michael Fogarty who was Professor of Industrial Relations and Sociology, a lay theologian and a very committed Catholic. He once asked me to give a talk on 'The Theology of Work'. This was a totally new concept to me, but I recognised that it was something we needed to be aware of and I set to researching the topic. The senior lecturer, George Thomason, oversaw my thesis. He was an Anglican, who knew Ireland well. 'The Church in Ireland has coped well with pastoral Ireland,' he once said to me. 'But how will it cope with industrial Ireland and the Ireland of new communications?' That really stuck in my mind. 'If the Church doesn't understand this changing Ireland now, it will never cope,' he added. 'That's why what you are doing is important.'

For my thesis I decided to look at the growth of cities in Britain from the period of the Industrial Revolution, beginning in the mid-nineteenth century. This coincided with the famine in Ireland. The Irish poured into these cities. They were initially housed in poor accommodation, often overcrowded, and eventually many moved into high-rise flats and huge housing estates.

One of these old communities in Cardiff was known as 'little Ireland'. It had a population of under one thousand people. Before I arrived, they had lost their priest. They were now to become part of the Cathedral parish. Living, as I was, in the presbytery attached to the cathedral, gave me the opportunity to get involved pastorally with this community.

The Cardiff Irish had come mostly from Cork – I could detect a similarity between the Cardiff and Cork accents! They were mostly the descendants of the Famine Irish. It was a community on the docks, cut off from the rest of the city by a railway track. The people who lived there were, for the most part, men who worked on the docks and their families. They never saw the sky over Ireland but they would passionately support the Irish rugby team against Wales at the nearby Cardiff Arms Park. As I got to know them, I grew very close to them and spent a lot of time with them, pastorally and socially.

I particularly remember the Burns family. There I was introduced to the novelty of toasted cheese sandwiches! Henry Burns was a natural leader of workers. He and his wife were marvellous homemakers. Their eldest son, Paul, was the first from the community to go to university. I took that little 'Irish' community as the focal group for my pastoral work and indeed research.

Living in the Cathedral parish, I sometimes met the Archbishop of Cardiff, John Murphy. He became very interested in the study I was doing and in the fact that a priest from a fairly rural diocese in Ireland had been sent to study sociology. He often talked to me about what I was doing.

The local council wanted to demolish some of the houses in that community and disperse the residents into estates around the city. A group, which included the residents, objected and tried to have community-led housing rebuilt in their place. The battle was lost, but I learned a lot from that experience. A seed had been sown in my head that when new housing estates are built the community dimension is vital.

My involvement with this community brought home to me how significant and practical the gospel message can be. As I got involved in the reality of life for people in the heart of this city, I became convinced of the importance of justice which is at the core of the Christian message. I had already started a study group with about fifteen dockers. We would meet once a week in a room over a pub to study the social encyclicals. These were hugely relevant to their lives, dealing with topics such as a just wage and the right to strike. On one occasion the dockers actually stopped a major strike, because they felt it would not be just. That, to me, was 'the Church in the modern world' in action.

I loved my time in Cardiff. It was a very open society – something I was not used to heretofore. I particularly befriended a PhD student who claimed to be an atheist. He and I agreed on a range of justice issues and especially on values which emphasised the importance of people – their dignity and their right to fair pay in the onward growth of an economy. I received my degree and was encouraged in the university to continue my studies. Professor Broady, attached to Swansea University, agreed to supervise me. However, Bishop Rodgers wanted me to get a wider experience with the Irish emigrants in Britain and so I put my studies on hold. I later published what I had written in a book called *Ireland Green*.

I now moved to the parish of Sparkhill in Birmingham. This was a parish of twelve thousand people, reputedly one of the biggest parishes in Britain. The people were mainly of Irish origin, with a parish priest and three curates to meet their spiritual needs. I arrived there on a Friday afternoon in 1965. The following evening, three fellows called to ask if I would hurl for the local club, John Mitchels. I said that I would but I had to warn them that I hadn't hurled for two years.

We went to Coventry on the Sunday to play a local team. I played at centre half-back and got a serious blow to the mouth. The mentors were very upset and wanted to take the young priest off but I played on. Afterwards, I was taken to hospital, where a young Limerick nurse insisted on stitching me without freezing my lip! I presented a sorry sight to the canon that evening in the presbytery. 'Don't tell me you play that barbarian game,' he remarked acidly. 'I do,' I said, 'but it's not barbarian.' He refused to let me say evening Mass. I continued to hurl for Mitchels. We never won anything but it was a way of keeping in touch with the people. That was really my job in Sparkhill – to keep in touch with emigrants. I don't think the canon ever fully appreciated that.

Birmingham was the centre of the motor industry so there were a lot of Irishmen working there, many of them bachelors, living alone and often turning to drink for company. The young women worked as nurses or on the buses. I could spend the whole day on pastoral work and then spend an hour or two at the weekends in the Harp dancehall where the young people danced to Irish showbands. I had two Masses on Sunday mornings in that same hall. This was another source of contact for me with the young Irish. Keeping in touch was important.

There were three curiae of the Legion of Mary who did marvellous work. My respect for the Legion grew enormously there. They were a prime example of the lay apostolate – lay people involved with basic Christian work. A big problem there was the shortage of accommodation for young couples. With a branch of the Legion, I got involved in trying to find a solution. We set up a Birmingham branch of the Catholic Housing Association, which Eamon Casey had established in London. This involved providing a facility for young couples to save regularly so that by the time they came to buy a house, they would have saved the deposit.

There was a tendency for young couples to go back to Ireland, spend their savings on the wedding and then come back to one room in Birmingham. A baby would arrive and the mother had to give up work and many, as a result, would be forever stuck in poor accommodation.

Drink and poor accommodation played havoc with family life. I remember being asked to mediate with a man who had been beating his wife. They lived in one room with five children. We talked. 'How would you feel having to live in conditions like these?' he asked. 'If you could get us decent accommodation, I am sure I could change my ways.' His comment really hit me. I realised that poor housing had an enormous impact on family life and that intolerable living conditions contributed hugely to many social problems. I clearly saw the need to work towards improving the quality of life of people like these, especially in the matter of housing and most especially of housing in a community setting. That family eventually made it home to Kerry.

On returning from a holiday at home, the canon told me that Fr Eamon Casey was looking for me. Eamon and the Catholic Housing Association were doing great work housing emigrants in London. Eamon knew me from my involvement in Birmingham. At his invitation, I went to meet him in London. He wanted me to get involved with him and suggested that I would come for a year to London with a view to developing the Housing Association. I said neither yay nor nay. Eamon flew to Shannon to ask my bishop, Michael Harty, to release me for ten years. Michael came over to England to meet emigrants. I drove him around the big cities. I told him I wasn't keen on the London job. 'Nor am I,' he said. 'I want you at home in the diocese.' Eamon was disappointed and asked me to change my mind. I stood firm – I was coming home to Clare.

I arrived back in Ireland in 1968 and was assigned to Shannon to work pastorally there but also with the freedom to explore the changes that were actually taking place, their impact on local communities and develop initiatives which would ensure that the two systems of family and community would not be neglected in the growth of an economy.

The Vatican II message through its document, *Gaudium et Spes* ('The Church in the Modern World'), made it clear that it was vital that the Church would face the economic, cultural, communications and education challenges which Irish people would be confronted with in the major changes that were taking place. The task facing the Church was to bring the Christian message to that society. I felt very strongly about this from the beginning.

When I was leaving Birmingham to catch the boat home, I brought with me Jack Tuohy, a Feakle man who was also returning home after a working lifetime away, and a greyhound pup that a Kilkenny man had given me! When the police stopped us, they were very suspicious – two men, a dog and a car full of cases and boxes – but they eventually let us go. Jack was a complete gentleman and liked a pint. There is a lovely story about him. A neighbour met him *resting* on his way home from the pub:

Neighbour:	The weather is up, Jack.
Jack:	How do you know?
Neighbour:	Well, the crows are settled on Neddy Nugent's hill.
Jack:	Sure they can't be flying all the time …

In a way, that could be a metaphor for my own concerns at the time – the need to be 'settled' in home and community. People, no more than crows, can't be flying all the time!

FOUR

The Social Encyclicals

The social encyclicals are the best attempts the Church has made to read the signs of the times, to identify the needs of the people and address them in accordance with Christ's teaching. They are among the most radical documents the Church has ever produced, but the message contained in them suffered seriously from failures in communication. The language was almost impenetrable and, therefore, seemed to have no relevance to life as lived by ordinary people. There was no attempt at any level in the Irish Church to decode it. This in particular applied to the earlier encyclicals. Catholic social teaching did not have a significant place in the curriculum of seminaries where dogma, moral theology, canon law and scripture, in that order, were prioritised. Further studies were largely confined to the fields of divinity and canon law. The fact that I had to go to the University of Wales, Cardiff to study sociology was, in itself, an indication of how poorly resourced the study of social issues was in both our Church- and State-led third-level institutions.

Many of us, as students, had an uncomfortable intimation that the curriculum offered to us had little relevance to life in places like Feakle, Shannon, Ennis or any of the towns and villages where we would work as priests. I had an increasingly strong appreciation of this as I progressed through Maynooth.

My interest in 'development' issues began with the experience of witnessing my classmates at school having to emigrate. Seeing at first-hand the growth of massive housing estates and high-rise flats and the implications for families led me to believe there has to be another way. But my interest in the social teaching of the Church and its relevance for an Ireland that was fast becoming industrialised and urbanised convinced me that it was right to get involved. Pope Paul VI described development as the new name for peace.

The first great social encyclical was *Rerum Novarum* – ('Rights and Duties of Capital and Labour'), issued by Pope Leo XIII on 15 May 1891. It focused on the modernity that had come with the post-Industrial Revolution. For the Church, the longest period of stability had been from the Middle Ages up until the Industrial Revolution. It had been a pastoral period, largely unchanging, and a time of great influence and power for the Church. Now all was changed. There was great migration to the cities, with the attendant problems of working conditions, housing and social justice. A new era of modern poverty had begun. The world was also moving away from the dominance of Rome, and Leo XIII recognised that. *Rerum Novarum* focused on the plight of the new poor and sought to create a moral and just society. It was critical of both capitalism and socialism and sought a third way to address the ills of the post-Industrial Revolution world by adopting a Christian approach to economic development.

Forty years later, in 1931, Pope Pius XI issued his encyclical *Quadragesimo Anno* ('Forty years have passed'). This introduced the principal of subsidiarity – that no greater body, e.g. the State, should perform functions that could easily be performed by a lesser body. This principle would later be adopted by the United Nations and, for me, it had major implications in the direction my life and work took subsequently. At the same time the Catholic Social Movement embraced vocationalism all over Europe. Here in Ireland the vocational school system was established to prepare young people for work in the trades and agriculture. As the twentieth century progressed, it became the century of institutional man and woman. Our lives were shaped by big organisations – the Church, the banks, State bodies. It was the beginning of globalisation. *Quadragesimo Anno* was not happy with this development.

In the 1960s, Pope John XXIII issued two encyclicals – *Mater et Magistra* ('Mother and teacher of all nations') in 1961 and *Pacem in Terris* ('Peace on Earth') in 1963, the year I was ordained. It was a period of great change for the Church. John XXIII had already convened the Second Vatican Council because he felt the Church needed to look at itself in the light of the changing world. It needed to speak words of hope. At the opening of the Council, he spoke these words: 'We feel we must disagree with those prophets of gloom who are always forecasting disaster.' He encouraged a focus on opportunities in the world for a balanced society. In *Mater et Magistra,* he expressed concern about the mass population movement to cities and the loss of balance in rural areas, the concept of community and the need for community to develop its own resources. Again he was harking back to *Quadragesimo Anno,* urging people to take responsibility for their own future. Rather than 'pontificate', John XXIII was encouraging the Church to facilitate. He was promoting a new kind of leadership.This was the era I emerged into as a young priest.

Later, Pope Paul VI in *Populorum Progressio* ('On the progressive development of peoples'), took up the theme of structural injustice. The central issue here was the lack of participation by people in determining their own lives. This indeed was the common thread running through all the social encyclicals and it influenced me greatly. If the Church were to make a serious contribution to the world, it would need to see that world through the eyes of the poor. Transformation would only come about by appealing to people of goodwill. Pope John Paul II in a further series of encyclicals continuously underlined the great scandals of poverty and deprivation in the midst of plenty.

The sixties was a decade of high optimism. There was a young Catholic president in the White House. The civil rights movement was gathering pace. In Africa, many states were being liberated from colonialism. In Ireland we experienced four revolutions – economic (Whitaker's 1958 Economic Development Plan had taken root), communications (television had arrived), education (Donogh O'Malley's free education scheme) and church (the completion of the Second Vatican Council). Great things were possible. Opportunities abounded, but sadly were not always grasped, nowhere more so than in the Church revolution.

Gaudium et Spes ('The Church in the Modern World'), 1965, is one of the great documents of the Second Vatican Council. Its key message was the importance for the Church of reading the signs of the times in a fast-changing world and interpreting these in the light of the gospel. How does Christianity affect citizenship and community, the interaction of Church and State, Christianity and the development of culture and the fostering of family life. Even today this document makes powerful reading:

> The Church wishes to enter into dialogue with the human family about the major issues that are happening in the world, about humanity's place and role in the universe and about the meaning of human life – individually and collectively. (#3)

The Council affirms its 'solidarity, respect and love for the whole human family of which it forms a part'. The Church seeks 'to be aware of and to understand the aspirations and the yearnings of people today'. (#4)

> We know that whatever contributes to the development of humankind on the level of family, culture, economic and social life ... according to the plan of God, also contributes to the life of the Church itself. (#44)

Development also contributes 'to the peace of the world and the prosperity of humankind' and 'help[s] permeate the world with the spirit of the Beatitudes'. (#72)

These to me were compelling, uplifting words. The Church was making it clear that the human person is the source of all economic and social life. This was far removed from the profit-driven market values of the global economic system. It was a powerful message – and it was largely ignored. The bishops came home from Rome. John Charles McQuaid basically told us there would be no great change, apart from major changes in the liturgy, with the introduction of the vernacular language. These changes were of course necessary but they ignored the question George Thomason had raised with me in Cardiff – 'How is the Church to connect with the new Ireland, this movement from a stable, pastoral Ireland?' That question needed to be faced but, except in isolated cases, there wasn't a willingness to meet this challenge. We have paid a heavy price for ignoring this question and it has contributed hugely to the Church becoming irrelevant to many in modern Irish society.

Looking back those post-Vatican II years were pivotal in shaping the future of the Church in Ireland. The changes which happened, for example in people's experience of the Liturgy, did not go deep enough. The refusal to engage with the changes envisaged by the Council left the Church unable to adapt to the major changes that were happening in Irish society. This was a lost opportunity for which the Church would pay a high price in later years.

By the time I had arrived back in Ireland in the late 1960s, industrial growth was the new phenomenon. As I had seen in the UK, development would bring a whole new set of issues and questions. I knew that the Church needed to be pastorally involved in this debate, using what influence it had to ensure that economic development would support and not destroy people, families and communities. I was fortunate that Bishop Michael Harty supported me in getting involved in these issues. Looking inward would not be an answer in an Ireland that was opening up to a wider world, influenced economically and socially by market values and secular influences. The power and influence of economic structures dominated by multinational corporations would be enormous. They would provide much needed employment but people, families and communities, should not be at their mercy.

FIVE

SOCIAL PLANNING

The major debate in Ireland in the late 1960s centred around social and economic planning and the shape that development would take. For the first time, planning was accepted as a major element in any organised approach to development in Ireland. This was a crucial debate that has had consequences which are still felt today.

The whole notion of economic development became a reality in Ireland in the 1950s. In the first 'plan for economic development' the author T. K. Whitaker, who was then Secretary General to the Department of Finance, claimed that in the Irish situation and in the circumstances (underemployment, mass emigration) prevailing at that time 'the overriding aim of planning is to put more people to work – producing competitively of course – so that total employment and total output will rise. This is the way to achievement of all our aims.' There is no doubt that this document gave direction to the new Irish approach to economic development. It was the foundation of broad policies at a centralised level and communicated downwards through organisations, such as the Industrial Development Authority and others which were centrally controlled. In the Irish situation it depended on one resource, namely capital, in order to attract export-oriented industry to the country. The major benefits were in the area of job creation, irrespective of where the jobs were to be created.

In fact, they were to be located in what was described as growth centres. The idea of growth centres was first introduced into Ireland in 1968 by planners, Buchanan and Partners, on behalf of the government. They suggested that nine centres should be identified. The main ones to be in Dublin, Cork and Shannon with some expansion taking place at other specified towns – six in all. The arguments put forward in favour of large-scale production and growth centres were based on a number of reasons, mainly economic, chief among them being the lower costs involved in some forms of concentration and with the possibility of a future spread effect. The Buchanan Report was undoubtedly the most comprehensive planning study ever published in Ireland. Perhaps no planning document ever published aroused so much controversy, most of which centred on concentration versus dispersal and the effects the strategy, if implemented, would have on rural areas.

I felt that these planning issues were crucial to the future shape of community in Ireland and to the kind of society we would become and so I got involved in this debate. My studies in Cardiff had enabled me to see that the model of development in the UK had led to major urbanised industrial centres with huge social problems. I hoped that we could avoid the same pitfalls here before we got too far down the industrialisation road. On returning to Ireland I continued to study social change in rural development supervised by Professor Maurice Brody. This gave me a language and a frame of reference against which I could develop my own thinking and address the issues we were now facing in Ireland. I was convinced that development in our context needed to be vastly different to the model employed elsewhere. It needed to take account of the unique settlement pattern which at the time was dominated by small villages, small towns and open countryside. By European standards Ireland had only two cities – Dublin in the East and Cork in the South. There was no doubt in my mind that there was a need to focus on small communities, indigenous resources, village centrality and the initiative and enterprise of individuals. This unique settlement pattern raised serious questions about the proposed model concentrating growth in a few centres.

In questioning the proposed 'growth centre' model, I was also drawing on a model of planning put forward in 1955 by François Perroux, the French economist whose work I had studied in Cardiff. The model of development proposed by Buchanan and others claimed to be, like Perroux's, a growth-centre model. However, Perroux had a very different concept in mind. Perroux's notion of a *growth centre* or *growth pole* meant sectoral growth, that is a spread of development under a range of headings, e.g. agriculture, mariculture, industry and services. For Buchanan and others the focus was almost exclusively on the growth pole of export-oriented industry, to the exclusion of other sectors. The Buchanan Growth Centre concept regarded the other sectors as suppliers of labour for export-led industry and saw the need to plan for centralised urban centres to house this labour force. This I was sure would create the same problems I had witnessed in the UK: massive housing estates, congested urban growth and rural depopulation with serious implications. Rural areas were not seen as having potential resources in their own right. There was obviously an urgent need for the promotion of overseas-sponsored manufacturing industry but not to the exclusion of a range of other developments. Had Perroux's model of sectoral development been implemented, it could have led to a much greater spread of development and the retention of the small settlement pattern – much more friendly to family and community stability.

There were other voices at the time who were also questioning a centralised planning model. The Limerick Rural Survey, initiated by Jeremiah Newman proposed that if we were to have balanced development in Ireland it would be necessary to make

> a careful examination into the pattern of Rural Centrality, of the human and non-human resources of

> the areas, of the existing and possible economic and social development of the area and of the financial and administrative adjustments which the effecting of such development would make necessary.

The Limerick Survey, which was regarded as a classic, pointed out that rural development cannot be left to the efforts of community organisations on their own. Newman stressed that the first and most important requirement for rural areas is the provision of jobs in selected towns. But this is not the only requirement. The provision of basic services, such as water, sewerage, electricity, telephones, postal services was also essential. Whilst recognising the progress which had been made by voluntary organisations in some of these areas, he felt that rural problems cannot be solved through national planning only. It is interesting to note that almost a half century later many rural communities are still deprived of some of these services.

Dr Liam Ryan, one of Ireland's leading social commentators, later to become Professor of Sociology in Maynooth, also commented significantly on the Buchanan plan:

> The Buchanan Report is a national plan where a regional plan is needed. As a national plan it would seem to be necessary. Already the fruits of the new economic philosophy would seem to be achieving in the area of job creation but meanwhile, the population continues to fall in the west and north-west. A little bit

> of dole here and a little bit of Bord Fáilte there will not be enough to change this trend. The people grumble but do nothing. But their grumblings have at least produced the beginnings of a sceptical scorn for any more of these half measures – each hailed successively as a messiah, each failing in turn – which litter the path of decline for the last 100 years.

Liam spoke these words in 1970. They are significant because they are suggesting that no amount of national programmes will ever solve local problems.

This debate on planning in which I cut my teeth over forty years ago is still as relevant today. The same questions keep coming up, issues I have struggled with and tried to move forward all my life.

In some ways that debate forced me to begin to articulate the vision I had for the future, the kind of society I wanted to work towards and the values which would underpin it. In the years since, my thinking has developed and deepened as has my conviction that social planning is as important as economic planning as well as my belief that the potential of local community, whether that be urban or rural, is still undervalued.

Back then, we put practically all our eggs into that one basket of export-oriented foreign industry and we are still doing the same today. Centralised decision-making which assumes that one cap fits all has proven disastrous for the multiplicity of small rural communities, their resources and people. There is still not nearly enough effort put into the concept of social planning.

Social planning must involve the maximum participation of people. Of primary importance is enabling people to solve their own problems, take responsibility for themselves as a basic principle, create jobs for themselves and become producers as well as consumers. Plans imposed from above can be frustrating for a large section of the population. Imposed plans and theories do not take account of the local situations. The ongoing half measures Liam Ryan referred to have led to a serious imbalance in the dispersal of population. The overpopulation of Dublin and surrounding areas is seriously out of line with any concept of balance. In Clare now almost half the population has been drawn into five or six parish communities to the detriment of thirty-six other communities within the county. These clearly indicate the lack of vision, the lack of a balanced approach to development, the lack of a system of local government with authority. This has impacted on a range of activities and services within these settlements – activities such as Gaelic Games, and services such as post offices and Garda barracks. The GAA for example has played an integral part in the life of these communities. However many are now forced to amalgamate with other parish communities in order to field teams. The closure of a number of service providers inevitably leads to further decline.

I was thinking about all this when a recent exchange of letters between Britain's Prime Minister David Cameron and Pope Francis in advance of the G8 summit was published. This exchange involved a 'a detailed analysis of what needs to be done to tackle the economic and political challenges faced by the world today'. In a reply to one of Mr Cameron's letters Pope Francis wrote to assert that the

> concern for the fundamental material and spiritual welfare of every human person is the starting point for every political and economic solution and the ultimate measure of its effectiveness and its ethical validity.

The Pope was arguing that economics must not rule.

In other words the Pope was clearly pointing out that social development is at least as important as economic development. The growth and development of industry linked to natural resources are vital to our future. Whilst a certain amount of progress has been made in recent years in the area of natural resources they have been seriously neglected in spite of the enormous potential in the food and marine industries, and in the natural skills of people themselves.

In a globalising world the local matters more and more. The local is about identity, it's about neighbour, it's about pride of place, it's about community. It's also about building from the ground up.

We have neglected this in the past. In the words of the famous Pete Seeger song, 'Where Have All the Flowers gone?' one could ask the question, 'Oh, when will they ever learn?'

SIX

THE WAY THAT I WENT

So here I was back in my native county. It was 1968. The year of student revolt across Europe. There was a quiet revolution underway in Ireland. Economic progress was evident all about us. I was thirty years of age and fired up with all those ideas from the social encyclicals and with the findings of my own study (mainly that building massive housing estates and high-rise apartments was not the way to go). We were putting all our eggs into one big and mainly multinational basket.

I was based at Shannon New Town, close to the airport. There were two thousand people living there at the time. It had just been established as a parish in its own right. Prior to that it was part of the parish of Newmarket-on-Fergus. It was here that the big changes were taking place and I had been sent to Cardiff to try to understand and interpret these changes. I was to be involved pastorally in this new parish but with the freedom to get involved in the change process. The late Canon Tim Mullaly was my parish priest and we got on well.

The Airport

The Airport at Shannon came into being as a refuelling stop for aeroplanes flying the Atlantic. In the mid-1930s sites for the airport were identified. In 1939 the first land-based aircraft landed at Shannon. Prior to this across the estuary the first flying boat landed at Foynes.

These were enormously significant developments for Ireland in the early years of independence and they placed Shannon and its airport in a key position as a hub for a whole range of developments in the following years.

It is generally accepted that many of these developments would never have taken place if it were not for the leadership of one man – namely, Brendan O'Regan. He was a local man, born and reared in nearby Sixmilebridge. As a young man he trained in hotel management and his first job was to manage the Falls Hotel, Ennistymon, owned by his father. The hotel catered for an influential clientele mainly from Dublin who came to play golf in Lahinch. Many of these would have been secretaries of government departments and others involved in the administration, growth and development of the country in its infancy as an independent nation. Through these contacts Brendan's qualities were recognised. He was then invited to rescue the Stephen's Green Club when it was about to go into liquidation. This was the venue in Dublin for social, political and business gatherings of many of these same clientele. After visiting Foynes for the opening of the

Flying Boats base Éamon de Valera arranged that the young O'Regan would move to manage the catering there.

In 1945 aviation and catering operations were transferred to Shannon. A public-private company was put in place with Brendan as manager. In the late 1940s the duty-free shop was established. In the early 1960s Shannon took off with the industrial free zone involving huge investments for American companies. At the time these companies were looking for bases across Europe. Shannon was in the right place at the right time and had the right manager and leader to avail of this. The first new town in the Republic followed. These were exciting times for Shannon, the surrounding counties and indeed the West of Ireland. The story is well-documented in the book *Ireland's Shannon Story* written by Brian Callanan and published in 1999.

Regional Planning

In 1968 Shannon became my home. I was fortunate at a very early stage to come in contact with Brendan O'Regan. An organisation called Sales and Catering ran the operation at Shannon for a number of years. Among the developments taking place was the opening of a training school for hotel management in 1951. A mail order department was opened.

In 1957 the Shannon Free Airport Development Company Ltd (SFADCo), now known as Shannon Development, was established – first as a management committee. This came about as a result of O'Regan convincing Sean Lemass that a civil service type structure was not appropriate for the development of Shannon. He argued that he himself should be given the job of developing Shannon and that a local company should be instituted to do it. In 1959 it was established as a limited company. Developments under the headings of Air Freight, Industry, Passengers, Tourism and Housing took place quickly.

In 1956, a jet runway was announced for Shannon. By now there was concern for the impact jet aircraft would have. The emergence of long-haul aircraft would eliminate the need for refuelling which would have a serious impact on passenger traffic. It was in the face of this challenge that Brendan emerged as a great leader. He simply refused to accept *no* from anyone.

When I arrived back in Shannon it had become a hub of activities and creative developments. True to form Brendan O'Regan had heard I had studied the impact of industrialisation in cities in Britain. He contacted me. In 1968 and 1969 SFADCo was given responsibility for planning regional industrial development. The region identified was Clare, Limerick and Tipperary North. Locations for industrial development in towns across the region were identified, advanced factories provided and promotion of these for the location of factories followed.

Brendan believed that it was essential that local people and voluntary organisations should be involved in this. As a result he asked Bishop Harty if he would agree to release me to get involved. Bishop Harty agreed but I was to continue to be involved pastorally in the new parish of Shannon.

The concept of people and planning became an integral part of the regional programme. Public meetings were held in centres across the region at which a few of the economists, the late Willie Moloney, Tom Kelleher, Tom Haughey and myself attended. These went on over two years and gradually a five-year programme for industrial development was produced, the first of its kind in Ireland with Shannon as the hub. Local people were consulted and involved in putting the programme in place. Gradually, I began to ask myself questions as to the impact of all this on small rural communities. Conflicting views emerged as to what regional development meant and was it to be confined to industrial development or should it have a broader interpretation.

A significant change occurred in the 1960s with the establishment of Aer Rianta as a new Irish Airports Authority. It was given responsibility for the management of Shannon Airport and so began a weakening of local control. Brendan O'Regan who was now chairman of the SFADCo board was finding it difficult to have the influence he had in earlier years. Control of the airport continued until 2012. It has now been handed back to local control. I use the example of the developments which took place at the airports, and the extension of its influence in other developments, to emphasise the importance of leadership and of local control.

Leadership is different from management and administration. Good leaders identify what they want to achieve. Managers involve themselves in the task of getting things done. Leaders are visionary, creative; they do not allow obstacles to get in the way of what they want to achieve. They involve themselves in change and transformation.

Brendan O'Regan's leadership qualities were responsible for most of the exciting developments at Shannon. That kind of leadership was essential at this time in Ireland. Local control as distinct from centralised power is essential if the transformation which is needed today is also to take place.

As time moved on Dublin control of SFADCo and the airport seriously undermined the Shannon project. Tom Kelleher, one of the economists involved in the regional dimension of the project would later say to me that failure to implement regional development in Ireland at that time was Ireland's great lost opportunity. How different Ireland would be now if it was implemented.

It is also worth mentioning how effective the role of SFADCo was. Whilst it had a certain degree of autonomy Brian Callanan points out in his book that between 1961 and 1986 there was a 102% growth in employment in the mid-west compared to a 20% growth nationally.

Over time, however, it lost its effectiveness. Sources outside the region, and especially Dublin sources, had become quite critical of its role of duplication with other agencies and indeed 'whether SFADCo was the appropriate body to promote Shannon'. There were critics from within too and it's fair to say that I was one of them. I parted from involvement with SFADCo in the early 1970s. I had come to believe that its response to local and community development needs was not appropriate and far too focused on the location of multinational companies. It seemed to me that the development of our local resources and our settlement pattern was being seriously undermined.

I acknowledge that SFADCo did much good but as time went on I also had some reservations about its approach to development. The early years of SFADCo were typified by getting the ideas first. Putting a structure on the ideas came afterwards. In later years, however, I felt the opposite happened. I watched SFADCo go through a period of being a structure without ideas, particularly in the sphere of regional industrial development.

For me the big question was whether SFADCo was involved in Regional Development or in Industrial location. I was disappointed that SFADCo was not looking more seriously at the resources of the region or the needs of rural areas. I believed that it got locked into industrial development instead of regional development. Once overseas industry stopped coming it did not seem to know what to do. In hindsight maybe it got so controlled by Dublin that it wasn't allowed. In later years it again made a serious effort to be more imaginative. For example it played a significant part in the development of Doonbeg Golf Course.

SFADCo no longer exists as an independent company. Part of it has been integrated into the new airport company. Local control of the airport is welcomed. This new company will obviously be involved in negotiating with airlines. For that it will need aviation expertise, good structures and management but it will also need good leadership, with a vision, creativity of the O'Regan era.

Shannon will always be different to other airports – it always has been. It is not and never was just about passenger traffic. Questions which will have to be asked now are: Why do people want to fly through Shannon? Why will passengers want to connect specifically with the west of Ireland? Why is the aviation expertise important now? What will be needed in the future?

Seventy million people worldwide claim an ethnic relationship with Ireland. Would it be worth considering a diaspora centre attached to Bunratty Folk Park. This could include links with the Famine, history of people and places from Donegal to Kerry, a museum, a replica of the workhouse in Ennis where thousands lived and died during the Famine. I know a certain amount of research has already been done on projects like this. In short, Shannon Airport will have a future when it's connected to the culture of the west of Ireland. Brendan O'Regan looked up to the skies and brought business down.

It's one thing being a critic of something. It's another to do something about it. I had become passionate about some elements of the development process. Some elements such as our settlement pattern, the systems of family and community were being ignored. I had also come to see the dangers of an agency such as SFADCo tending almost to become an end in itself. My involvement in the local Church and Shannon new town through all this time made me very aware of community breakdown, depopulation in many of the small communities and I was also becoming very aware that we were beginning to make the same mistakes which were made in Britain after the industrial revolution. We were building massive housing estates and high-rise flats in places like Limerick City. It was obvious to me then that this was not the way to go.

SEVEN

Rural Resource Organisation

The villages and local communities were never far from my thoughts and I began to think about what could be done. After a lot of soul-searching I got the idea of building houses in villages for young families who were being forced to move to the bigger centres. Prior to doing anything I examined the settlement pattern in the mid-western region.

In order to understand why it was important to challenge the concentration of people as well as the bulk of industry I felt the typical settlement pattern of Irish counties should be noted and taken account of. For example, in the early 1970s the mid-west region contained almost one hundred and forty settlements ranging in size from a large centre like Limerick City to crossroad villages comprising only a few houses.

The Limerick Rural Survey, referred to earlier, carried out by Jeremiah Newman showed the geographical distribution of settlements, cities, towns and villages. This showed a definite pattern. The spacing of towns was roughly fifteen to twenty miles apart and about eight miles between the village centres. Historically, villages emerged from the need to provide services to an agricultural population which found it convenient to live in scattered homesteads on the farms.

Whilst there were and are certain variations in the settlement pattern of villages and towns the spatial structure of the typical Irish rural scene is fairly simple. It is made up of scattered homesteads around a small village. The villages are small and numerous and so limited in the amount of services they provide. Most villages have or had a school, a church, a Garda station, a pub(s) and a grocery shop(s). These are multiplied according to size. The towns and bigger villages had a variety of shops and possibly a bank and a secondary and / or a vocational school.

The most important study which has been made of the Irish countryside is that carried out in North Clare in the 1930s by Arensberg and Kimball entitled, *Family and Community in Ireland*. These authors attach the main significance to two elements of human organisation, as implied in the title:

> The sociology of Irish Rural Life and small farm subsistence is barely a matter of the anatomy of two institutions of characteristic form. They are the family and the community. Together these two unite essentially all the persons of the rural areas.

They saw these two acting as a framework of relationships around which custom moved. These included social, economic, religious, sporting and cultural customs. They are the two systems which held generations of Irish people together.

Other studies carried out in the 1960s emphasised the certainty of the family farm and the importance of neighbours. One of these was carried out in Bansha, Co. Tipperary by members of the Agricultural Advisory Service, 'Community Development and Agricultural Extension Services' (Paper by Dr H. Spain, 1962). In his report of this study, Dr Spain pointed out:

> In Ireland, we do not have the farm villages typical of many European Countries – farm families are scattered throughout the countryside. This relative isolation results in many small informal groups of neighbouring farm families.

Nine distinct neighbourhoods were identified in the parish. So in a sense Bansha, as was the case with other parishes, was and is a community of communities. (This became very clear to us in Sixmilebridge and Kilmurry which led us to initiate our 'area gatherings', described later in the book.) Other studies such as that carried out by Hugh Brody (*Inishkillane: Change and decline in the west of Ireland,* Allen Lane, 1973) dealt with the impact of emigration and especially with the level of demoralisation which followed.

The population decline which weakened the rural areas eventually effected the villages. By the end of the 1950s they were losing a large proportion of the younger age group, resulting in a serious age imbalance.

I looked at my native village, Feakle, less than twenty miles from Shannon. In 1970 it had a population of one hundred and twenty, only three of whom were in the twenty to forty age group. Others in that age group had migrated. An age group which had emigrated in the 1940s and 1950s were now migrating to the bigger centres at home. Jeremiah Newman's words proved almost prophetic:

> The possibility is a real one that the future may see Ireland as a prosperous nation with a favourable balance of trade and little emigration but with its people packed into a few huge cities and provincial centres and its countryside a prairie; very sparsely populated by wealthy farmers but haunted by the ghosts of dead towns and villages.

For some reason I had a conviction that this did not have to be. It was time to think 'outside the box'. A bureaucratic approach to development was obviously concerned with growth but not with the spread of that growth taking account of the settlement pattern peculiar to Ireland. I found myself giving a lot of thought to this. I also found myself attending meetings in rural halls where people were seriously concerned about population decline in their areas. The dominant instrument of growth at the time was industrial, large companies, advanced factories – in a few centres. I felt if this approach could be reversed, namely housing for young families who could commute through quiet roads to the nearest growth centre then other developments could follow in these communities connected with natural resources and small industries. It would also be taking account of the creation of a healthy environment for families, the formation of communities, connection of people not only to one another but also with creation, and with the greater appreciation of a God as Creator.

Furthermore, I had come to believe that coming one hundred years after the Industrial Revolution in Britain, Ireland, now experiencing its own mini-revolution, had a wonderful opportunity to redefine the concept of growth in terms of people and the units of family and community which shape them. It was obvious with the growth of communication technology, transport, etc., that development could start by ensuring that our settlement pattern would be taken into account. This could be based on concepts such as a Christian view of economic development and the concept of 'small is beautiful'.

So having come up with the idea of providing houses for young couples in villages I went to discuss the idea with a man called Johnny Mee, who was the local bank manager in Shannon. From the outset Johnny was enormously supportive. The basic idea was to set up an organisation which would encourage young couples to save for a deposit which would in turn help to develop a saving habit. In conjunction with this a small voluntary group was put together, comprising people with expertise in the building of small schemes of houses.

Johnny himself agreed to be part of the group which in the early days included an architect, an accountant, an economist and the manager of a big construction company.

We decided we would start in Feakle. I said to myself at an early stage – If we can't do it in Feakle, we can't do it anywhere! We held a meeting to put the proposal to the people. That night confirmed a lot. It was a very animated meeting. The people of Feakle felt they had been written off as a community. Some of the experts told us that people would not go back to live in villages anymore. However, the people themselves were clearly indicating the opposite.

We asked the parish priest to announce at Sunday Mass that young couples who would like to live in Feakle should come to the hall on the following Friday night. This seemed crazy at that time. For a start, who were we? However, representatives of twenty families came to the hall on that Friday night. The concept of a rural housing organisation was born.

This became our *modus operandi*: We met young couples and got them to save £20 a week towards a deposit which would in turn enable them to borrow from the banks, local authorities, building societies.

With a lot of hard work, cajoling and persuading, twenty houses were built, which nearly doubled the population of the village. In 1973, the then Taoiseach Liam Cosgrave came to open them. Michael Harty blessed the houses and a new hall on the same day. Some people thought we were crazy. We were running counter to the thinking of centralised growth. Maybe that was the economic way forward but it wasn't the social way. I really believed in the model we were proposing. The late Con Smith built a hotel in Feakle, something unheard of previously. The school got an extra teacher. We had created our own growth centre but with the emphasis on people – family and community.

Other villages like O'Callaghan's Mills and Bodyke were interested. A company was formed and the RHO took off. People might have been living close to growth centres where they worked, but they were not benefitting greatly from them. My argument was that if big industrial estates were needed to house factories, we didn't need big housing estates to house people. They could be dispersed in villages which could provide smaller communities, face-to-face contact, informal relationships and opportunities for mutual self-help. The RHO eventually spread across Ireland, ultimately building two thousand five hundred houses in one hundred and twenty villages in thirteen counties from Cavan to Cork.

Through the RHO, ten thousand people established homes in small communities, many of them bringing their skills with them. Some of these, in turn, set up small enterprises. In bringing back people in the twenty to forty age group, the impact was soon visible in other things:

- Average village populations increased by 30%.
- Rural schools expanded instead of closing.
- Community centres and village hotels were built.
- Small industries were generated.
- New shops opened.
- Emigrants returned to their local areas.
- Transport, water and sewerage services improved.
- Other houses were built – professional services were provided – doctors, chemists, etc.
- Young farmers were more inclined to stay on farms (when their own age group returned).

A key aspect of the RHO was the involvement of the community from the beginning. Johnny Madden, the Contracts Manager, and I would go into a village on invitation only. The local community identified housing land and the demand for houses – they were involved from day one. All this time I was promoting, through writing and media appearances, a view of economic development, which for me linked with the gospel. The late John Healy, the well-known journalist with *The Irish Times* and the *Western People*, described the work of the RHO as 'modern patriotism' in the *Western People*. We never saw ourselves as 'modern patriots' nor perhaps did we fully appreciate the impact the RHO would have. For me it was a practical thing. I didn't want to be a romantic with unworkable ideas. For me they *had* to work. Otherwise industrialisation was a major threat to family and community life, and if they fractured, society in general was at risk.

In the west of Ireland we always seemed to be begging for grants to start up industries when the reality was that money from the west was being channelled through the banks out of the west to be invested elsewhere. This seemed crazy to me. About this time, I came across the idea of a people's bank which had originated in nineteenth-century Germany. In this instance, money deposited in an area would stay in that area and be invested there. I discussed it with T.J. Maher, ex-president of the Irish Farmers' Association and now President of the Irish National Co-operative Society, and he was very supportive of the idea. We developed the idea of forming a bank with the help of the Catholic Church, co-operative and farming organisations, etc. However, when we explored the idea further with an economist from the Central Bank, who explained how many millions of pounds we would need, I realised we were way out of our depth! Nevertheless, we decided to proceed on a smaller scale and approached the bishops for low-cost borrowing that we could loan out to small business projects. We raised £100,000 in that way and got twenty-eight small projects going. In every single case the borrowings were paid back in full.

The Rural Housing Organisation had now become the Rural Resource Organisation (RRO). Our aim had gone beyond housing to developing local natural resources. We planted seeds in different ways. We gathered a group of people who would facilitate small groups in villages – old and new residents – to get involved in fireside chats on topics such as living in the home, living in the community, identifying local resources, etc. A group would come together around the fire in a village to discuss community life. A leader would introduce a topic – maybe the setting up of a co-operative for vegetable growing – and facilitate discussion. Someone else would lead the following week's gathering. Growth in resource development came from those meetings. Dr Tom Collins worked on integrating those ideas into the world of education. In preparing people for an economy, education tended to follow rather than lead. We had great assistance from Diarmaid Ó Donnabháin, the Principal of Shannon Comprehensive School at the time, who pioneered many interesting projects.

For me the day was not long enough. I was writing about these ideas, talking to school principals, speaking to fellow priests (at the time I was being asked to give retreats all over the country). I was also President of the National Council of Priests in Ireland. We priests were examining the role of the priest in modern Ireland, in the hope that the real experience of priests in ministry would be taken on board in the preparation of future priests.

The response of county managers to the RRO was very mixed. Men like the late Dick Haslam in Limerick and Michael Duignan in Roscommon were supportive but at times we met with negativity and an unwillingness to work with an approach from the ground up. There were times when financially we sailed far too close to the wind. We had to install water and sewage services and the county council was then expected to take these over, but in many cases they did not. This became a massive burden on the organisation. The Minister for the Environment, Pádraig Flynn, once said to me – 'Why did you set up that organisation? If the West is dying, I'll save it!' i.e. leave it to government, not voluntary organisations. In fact government bodies taking over from community-development organisations did serious damage at that time. Government would roll out a few big projects in big places with a lot of publicity, but rural areas were continuing to die. In fairness to Minister Flynn, he did give £100,000 to local government to take over sites from us.

The downturn in the economy in the 1980s hit us hard. We had acquired a bank of land which we couldn't use. RRO's time had run out. We sold off the land, paid our bills and by the end of the decade we had £3,000 left in the bank. I was disappointed that neither Church nor State picked up on our ideas. We had set up the RRO to demonstrate that the way forward was in small steps – a la John XXIII in *Mater et Magistra* and Schumacher in *Small is Beautiful*. Government could only do big things in big places; it could never see that the way forward was to facilitate people to take responsibility for their own lives. The same could be said of the Church.

On the positive side, we brought people back into the villages and kept them out of big growth centres. We extended the web of rural development. Social life was regenerated. The GAA benefitted greatly – it was a matter of great pride to me to eventually see that eleven out of fifteen players on the Feakle under-14 team came from 'rural houses'.

I was approached by Phillip Lowe, a high-ranking European executive in Brussels, to write a paper on rural development, based on my experiences with RHO and RRO. The depopulation of rural areas was becoming a problem across Europe. I pointed out to him that rural development was about a mix of economic, social and cultural activities. In contrast, growth-centre development was purely economic. I put my ideas on paper for him and I would like to believe that it helped formulate the thinking behind the LEADER programme – the EU's response to previously ineffective ways of tackling rural depopulation in peripheral regions. To be a part of this move in Clare, RRO evolved into Rural Resource Development Ltd – a partnership of all the significant actors in the rural development endeavour – RRO, Teagasc, Golden Vale Co-op Marts Ltd, Clare Marts Ltd and various community-based organisations. This unique initiative would provide, in its structure and philosophy, an unqualified commitment to a 'bottom-up' approach. It was about power returning to the people.

Postscript
In May 2012 I received this letter from Zambia. Perhaps the seeds sown in 1970s Ireland are now being transplanted in Africa.

Society of African Missions Zambia
16 May 2012

Dear Harry,

I am an S.M.A. priest working here in Zambia for the past twelve years. Before I was ordained way back in 1977 you were one of the priests who gave me inspiration and also since my ordination because of your work with the Shannon housing project for young married couples. I had known of you because of your passionate involvement with the Clare hurlers through my cousin Gus Lohan and Seán Stack, a former teammate on Maynooth Fitzgibbon teams. However it was your self-help style of development that I found most inspiring.

You will be happy to know that I have extended your development idea to a small township here in Kitwe, Zambia.

We have a small housing project for ex-street children and vulnerable women, widows and those living with HIV Aids. It is called 'Twafwane' housing project which in the local language means 'helping ourselves'. The project was started in 2008 and since then we have built 42 decent houses consisting of two bedrooms, a sitting room, kitchen and bathroom. Our target is to complete 64 houses by September 2013. Of every ten houses built three must go to ex-street kids.

So far the project is going very well with the local community very much involved in the digging and laying of foundations, carrying mortar, bricks, water, painting and brickmaking. Youth, mostly from the street, have been trained in block-making and building. We are modelling our efforts on the Habitat for Humanity style where we provide the materials as a loan and the new homeowners repay the equivalent of one bag of cement per month over a ten-year period. Their repayments are intended to create an evolving fund for future development. The new homeowners are so proud of their efforts and are the envy of many of their neighbours.

I hope your own efforts at development continue to bear fruit.

Wishing you God's blessings,
Fr Anthony Kelly S.M.A.

EIGHT

A Note on the Family Farm

The concept of the family farm is central to rural development. Down through the centuries, it has been a central part of our connection with the land. The whole family was involved in what happened on the farm. Work and home were closely connected. The farm was a place of learning and tradition. I grew up in the 1940s and 1950s in a community of small farmers and shopkeepers. I felt a deep affinity with people and place in a geographical sense (we knew the names of fields, farms and townlands) and in a cultural sense. So when I got involved in community and rural development, I became convinced that the recovery of a real relationship with the land was vital. Unfortunately, this was at a time of mass migration from the land for jobs in factories and offices.

Milk production was central to the stability of the family farms. In 1984 quotas on milk production were introduced by the European Union. At that time over fifty per cent of milk producers were classified as small scale. In Co. Clare, there were over three thousand five hundred active milk producers, half of them being regarded as small-scale producers. As many of them ceased production, their quotas were bought by large producers in other parts of the country. The loss of such a vital resource did not make much sense in the context of rural development.

Jerry O'Connor (RIP), Michael McGrath, the then Chief Agricultural Officer for Co. Clare, and myself got to thinking and talking about this. Michael was an imaginative, creative and courageous public servant, for whom the concept of voluntary and statutory bodies working together made sense. He had a similar outlook to Johnny Mee from the banking world who got involved in the rural housing initiatives. Michael and I got in touch with Professor Joe Mannion, head of the Agricultural faculty in UCD. Joe was an academic who had a practical application built into the education and research programmes run by his faculty. Together we discussed the importance of retaining milk production and milk quotas in small rural communities. It was agreed to carry out a study of milk quotas in Co. Clare in 1993.

In the ten years prior to the study, approximately one thousand two hundred farmers had ceased dairying. There were now two thousand three hundred suppliers in Clare. The study found that one-third of these would cease milk production soon after the study was completed. Another third would need substantial government aid to carry on. Seventy-five per cent of existing farmers would have to invest in facilities to meet EU milk quality standards. The study recommended government grants for modernisation and the purchase of quotas. It also recommended that government policy should change towards targeting additional quotas for small-scale producers who could expand their operations. Further, Teagasc (the farm advisory body) should provide extra advisory support to dairy farmers at both individual and group levels. These groups became an important way forward towards farmers' acquisition of the skills and knowledge needed for the development of their farms.

The study recommended a pilot milk quota restructuring scheme for Co. Clare. Subsequently, a national scheme gave priority to small-scale producers in the distribution of quotas. Quotas were now ring-fenced in disadvantaged areas. Any farmer selling his milk quota in Co. Clare could now expect that it would be purchased by another Clare farmer. As a result, the amount of milk produced in the county in 2012 is the same as in 1993, the year of the study. The study proved that values, other than economic and market, must be an integral part of development programmes. It was also clear that the voluntary sector with on-the-ground local leadership could have a major input in development programmes, thus ensuring the participation of people with a lived experience of needs. This was a clear example of the 'principle of subsidiarity' highlighted by the social encyclicals of the Catholic Church, i.e. no higher power should assume control of initiatives which can best be carried out at a local level.

Liam and Maureen Meehan were typical of the people involved in the milk study. They were married in 1978 and started dairying with nine cows. They lived in a mobile home beside the old farmstead for eight years. During those years they extended the house and their dairy enterprise. They used low-cost techniques, new at the time, to expand their herd. Those of us involved in rural development built a training centre next to their house. Thousands of farmers came from Ireland and abroad to study the Meehans' methods. Two of their sons acquired farms with dairy herds and their solicitor daughter now works from the home, advising on the methods and structures which will help prospective young farmers.

Sadly, I write this having just returned from celebrating Maureen's funeral Mass. She died from cancer at the age of fifty-eight. At the Mass I quoted one of her sons, who told me – 'Maureen was the engine of the family, Liam the turbo and we were the wheels.' Maureen was a true spiritual leader. She had vision and spirit and worked with Liam and their children as a family unit to bring about interesting developments in family farming.

The family farm concept, rural community development, community ownership of the local mart, parish pastoral initiatives, prayer and spiritual initiatives – all are part of going back to first beginnings, to Christ Himself, for guidelines in the work of the priest and the Christian community.

NINE

The Family

From a very early stage in my life, and indeed right through my ministry, I was aware of the centrality of the family to life and living, to growing up, to relationships, to being the real school of learning and the real foundation for values. The family unit and the local community were the two key systems which formed and bound people together for generations. They had remained static and unchanging for decades, the main challenge coming from emigration. Such was the toll taken by emigration that there were parts of the west of Ireland in the 1980s that had no families left.

The pace of change from the 1960s onwards had a significant impact on the family. This in part led to the founding of the Rural Housing Organisation and later the Rural Resource Organisation. I have always been impatient with thoughts, comments, and analyses that are not followed by action. Too many policy documents and planning decisions are overly informed by theorists and theory and too little by action and reality. Coupled with that impatience was a frustration with those forces which prevent 'ordinary' people from realising their full potential. For most of my life I have been a 'doer', involved in initiatives based on practical visions. Hence my involvement in the RHO and the RRO.

If we take a brief look at the family in twentieth-century Ireland, the family of the earlier half had certain obvious features. In rural Ireland especially, it was dominated by the father, often referred to as 'the boss'. Sons, even into middle age, were given little authority and were still referred to as 'the boys'. The mother was responsible for feeding and clothing the children and for their emotional life. The family was very much a production unit, with clear sets of male and female tasks and within which children played an important part. Older children had their specific jobs to do and worked alongside their parents inside and outside the home. It was a kind of apprenticeship education.

Marriages were often 'arranged'. The 'match' was a common form of marriage in rural Ireland. In a society where physical survival was a constant preoccupation, marriage was very much a social and economic vehicle for that survival. As K.H. Connell put it, 'marriage was likely to be contemplated not when a man needed a wife, but when the land needed a woman'. Practically every family had a range of adults associated with it – grandparents, unmarried uncles and aunts, hired help, neighbours and close friends. Recreation centred around conversation with them. Children listened and a big threshold was crossed when they were eventually allowed to join in. Grandparents were especially honoured and wielded power. The whole family was conscious of its dependence on God. Prayer was important, necessary, habitual. Praying *together* was vital, the togetherness was as important as the prayer. Statues and pictures of the Sacred Heart were very much part of the home. Likewise the weekly Mass was as important as a community gathering as it was as a people at prayer.

It would be wrong to over-romanticise this bygone era. The circumstances were totally different to what came later. Parental influence was strong and a sense of responsibility and worth was inculcated from an early age. The home was a place of learning where members shared work, prayer and leisure. Because future occupational roles were largely unchanging, parents thought more about their children's characters than about careers – will they be honest and honourable? Can we count on them to respect us in our old age?

The roots of change in the family go back to the 1960s. Industrialisation and urbanisation brought new levels of prosperity. The family was now much more a consumer unit than a producer. There was the beginning of a revolution in communications technology, especially with the advent of television and telephone. The pattern of a three-generational household went into decline, which radically changed the position of old people. The number of nuclear and single-parent families grew. As the position of the father declined, that of the woman of the house underwent a long overdue change. She questioned her traditional role in the family. She challenged the arranging of marriages and the legal inequality that had made her subservient for life. With their newfound freedom, women changed the traditional family as it evolved in the second half of the twentieth century.

In the 1950s Ireland had the lowest marriage rate in Europe and very high celibacy rates – one in four women and one in three men aged fifty-five and over were unmarried. Average marriage age was thirty-three for men and twenty-eight for women. By 1980 that had dropped to twenty-seven for men and twenty-four for women. Modern marriage was making great demands on relationships and marriage failure was a growing reality. For young people these societal changes meant that they had only a limited range of real-life relationships with grown-ups. This underlines the importance of sport for young people, as coaches, trainers and managers may be the only adults with whom they can have a close relationship, which fosters character formation, mental toughness and self-belief.

The popularity of television also presented children with an array of authoritative adult figures which often posed problems for their relationships with their parents. Finally, the emergence of secularism and individualism had further implications for the family, leading to a dependence on outside organisations (e.g. the State) accompanied by disenchantment and isolation. Thus over the space of a few decades the family has moved from being a self-sufficient and relatively independent unit to one of increasing dependency. The challenge now is to identify the current situation of the family, what its needs are and how the local community can reconnect with it in responding to those needs. Hence, understanding the changing pattern of family life in Ireland was an area of primary concern for the annual Céifin conferences.

In 2003, Céifin promoted a major piece of research entitled 'Family Wellbeing – What Makes a Difference?' The entire conference of 2008 concentrated on different aspects of family life in Ireland. By that time we had become a nation of high spenders, high borrowers and conspicuous consumers. Family relationships suffered. The shopping centre became the social outlet for many families on Sunday afternoons. Financial pressures, driven by the need to maintain a bloated lifestyle, left couples with little time or energy for family or community life. And then in 2008 it all came crashing down about us.

This is not to say that the economic boom was unwelcome. It was welcomed with open arms and it gave Ireland a new standing internationally. However, we lost sight of the important values and blew the opportunity to create the balance between economic success and a healthy family life. Now family and community, once the glue that held Irish society together for generations, will have to provide the creativity, leadership and vision for the future of that society.

Change will not come from the top but from a mobilised grassroots who will have to be given responsibility and be facilitated to achieve that change.

So the big question is – how resourceful are family units after a period of consumerism? Can they be facilitated to make the required sea change into the future?

With these questions in mind, and a felt need to understand the needs of families after the boom and now the bust, Céifin is presently sponsoring a study on *The Impact of Societal Change on the Family Unit*. The study is focused on two communities: one urban, one rural, both in Co. Clare. It aims not only to name the factors which are impacting, both negatively and positively, on family today but to also identify specific, feasible responses, at local community level, to support family life. It is intended that the conclusions drawn from the study and the recommendations made will result in specific initiatives. These local community supports and initiatives would complement the services provided directly or indirectly by the State at a time of ever-decreasing public funding.

The study is still in the process of finalisation but an interim report has given some indication of the kind of issues that are surfacing. Among the major issues are those of isolation and disconnection, experienced differently in rural and urban settings. The breakdown of the traditional family unit is evident as is the difficulty experienced by families who are not Irish integrating into community. Another cluster of issues arise from the impact of the collapse of the economy and the uncertainty about its recovery which has resulted in families dealing with high levels of financial debt, unemployment, and fears for the future. Many respondents expressed a fear that their children would have to emigrate, for example. Significant too is the impact of issues of loss and bereavement on family life and a finding of an absence of support during these crucial times.

The study is due to be completed by the end of 2013. It will give us a picture of the reality of family life in the middle of one of the worst recessions this country has known. And perhaps most importantly, it will suggest some specific responses that could offer support.

TEN

The Coming of Céifin

By the late 1990s the Irish economy and Irish society were undergoing a dramatic transformation. The Celtic Tiger brought unprecedented economic growth with a marked increase in prosperity and material well-being. It was a growth whose impact did not touch all geographical areas or social groups, but it was still welcome. We came to be the best-housed, best-schooled, clothed and fed people ever to have lived in Ireland, with employment rates at an all-time high. We were an affluent society, part of a global economic system. Big corporations were the engines that drove most aspects of political, social and economic life. However it was also becoming increasingly obvious to some people that our society was beginning to pay a high and unacceptable price for our material prosperity.

In the headlong rush to identify ourselves with what we owned rather than who we were, we were losing sight of the very core of society – people, place, roots, soul. There was a need for debate to identify the values which could restore the balance in our lives. As we approached a new millennium it was time to ask major questions. What kind of society do we really want?

Where do our values come from? Who or what gives meaning to life? And so in 1998 Rural Resource Development convened a conference in the West County Hotel in Ennis under the challenging title – 'Are We Forgetting Something?' In other words, let us take time out to look at where we are and what direction our society is taking. Are we happy with it or are we indeed forgetting important things?

For three days, a succession of speakers carried this debate to a very high level. An attendance of five hundred people from a broad cross-section of Irish society – business, education, caring professions, local authorities, students – indicated that we had tapped into something important. Professor John Drew from Durham University set the tone:

> The (coming) millennium is a time of great opportunity for our planet ... A new year gives cause for reflection, a hundred years even more so. A millennium is something altogether different, especially as it falls by chance in the middle of three or four decades of the most profound changes our planet has ever witnessed.

Ireland was only a few years into a period of extraordinary change as a nation, as families and as individuals. We were racing ahead economically at a very fast pace and borrowing heavily at all levels. It was all *boom* – and nobody from government down was daring to think of or mention *bust*, except maybe economist David McWilliams, who addressed the conference on 'boom to bust' in economic history. He forecast our impending doom with chilling accuracy:

> We have the Tiger economy which everyone eulogises about. This attracts capital flow, because everyone wants a slice of the action. Interest rates come down very, very quickly. Punters start buying houses. People begin to believe their own propaganda … Banks get in on the action and start lending money hand over fist. The government, flush with tax revenue, decides to cut taxes … People borrow even more and begin to live astride a debtor's bubble. The final phase moves us into the real nonsense stage. Too many cars appear, followed by jams … Wages rise in certain sectors and asset prices go even higher … Just when everyone is having a great time and the party is in full swing the global recession, which has been building, hits us. The lights go out.

This was said in 1998, remember. And what would happen next, according to David McWilliams …

- The labour market would suffer first. Many jobs especially in the service industries would be lost and emigration would rise.
- If house prices crashed, negative equity would be a common feature.
- It was possible that one of the banks would fail.
- The national budget surplus would quickly turn to deficit and 'we could move from being the darlings to being the dunces of the EU very quickly'.

David was immediately branded 'a prophet of doom', but he was in fact a prophet who should have been listened to by the government, by the banks, by all of us.

That Ennis conference, which would run annually for eleven years, had in its very first gathering become a vehicle for looking at the signs of the times and identifying key issues which we as a society were forgetting. And it wasn't just the harsh outer economic world that concerned us. We as conference founders were conscious that the contemplative world had much to say to the new Ireland. A group of us visited the Poor Clare convent in Ennis, exchanged ideas with the sisters, prayed with them, listened to their wise, reflective views and were delighted when their superior, Sr Thérèse, agreed to address the first conference:

> Condemn me if you will for my simplicity, but it is my firm belief that society is dispirited and disillusioned, because by and large, we are living 'outside of ourselves' … As Carl Jung puts it, 'Your vision will become clear only when you can look into your heart; who looks outside, dreams, who looks inside, awakes …'

Sr Thérèse was right. The spiritual dimension of life had been seriously eroded in Celtic-Tiger Ireland. A growing number of people were searching for meaning, but the Church did not seem able to respond effectively to them. Mark Patrick Hederman reminded us that we need to face the darkness within us:

> We are made up of shadow and light ... One of Ireland's tasks in the Europe of the next century must be to remind ourselves and remind all Europeans that we carry the dark around with us, that it is an essential part of our make-up, that we never shake it off and move onwards ...

We were really blessed in our choice of speakers at the first conference. President Mary McAleese opened the conference:

> We have a long and proud tradition of community activity in Ireland. We take great pride in our origins and our sense of loyalty to the people and the place from which we come. It is not at all surprising that this should express itself in concern for the common good in the form of voluntary and community service ... this commitment is even more relevant and valued today ...

John Lonergan spoke from the heart as Governor of Mountjoy Prison in identifying 'the symptoms of a soulless society':

> My vision for the new millennium is of a society which is caring, compassionate, forgiving and sensitive to the needs of all our people, a society where people's needs come first.

Professor Joe Lee echoed the vision in his paper 'A Sense of Place in the Celtic Tiger?':

> A sense of place implies belief in an inclusive society where the weak are cherished as much as the strong. How far it will be sustained in the Ireland now emerging depends partly on factors beyond our control in an age of globalisation. But it also depends largely on how we choose to respond to globalisation. It means influencing, if not capturing, the commanding heights of opinion formation. It means a conscious attempt to build institutional structures, especially educational ones, that keep open the possibility of viable communities outside the metropolis and equally importantly, within it.

Further contributions from David Begg and Mary Redmond emphasised the importance of (a) civil society acting collectively to influence the quality of life and (b) voluntarism providing the alternative vision that is needed to complement the information society. We can influence the direction in which we go.

When the conference ended, after three days of highly-charged debate and discussion, there was a palpable buzz among the five hundred delegates. Are we forgetting something, indeed. They would carry the emerging issues back to their workplaces, schools, communities – issues such as:

- Understanding the nature of change.
- Reawakening the inner dimensions of our lives.
- Understanding the influence of the global economy and of the media.

- The rediscovery of the local – people, places, belonging, community, roots.

They asked if there would be another conference in 1999. Yes there would. The debate was only beginning. Likewise the search for values which would restore the balance in our lives.

We spent some time looking for a name for this new quest. Eventually the name *Céibhfhionn* was suggested. Céibhfhionn was the Celtic goddess of inspiration. We modernised the name to Céifin. That wise man John Drew had quoted the writer Saint-Exupéry – 'As for the future, your task is not to foresee, but to enable it.' We in Céifin would strive to enable a values-led future for Irish society – a society that certainly needed inspiration.

ELEVEN

The Flourishing of Céifin

Buoyed by the success of the 1998 conference, we began planning for the next conference whose theme would be 'Working Towards Balance'. We were, however, working on very slim resources. Some initial funding from the ESB enabled us to put a small staff in place. We identified five main areas for consideration:

The Corporation and the Community
We put a framework in place to establish ways in which corporations could form links with communities. Waterford Glass and Nortel (Galway) became involved in this project.

The State of the Family in Ireland
An advisory group was established and major research on 'Family well-being – what makes a difference?' was carried out by Kieran McKeown, a social and economic research consultant and his team. Funding came from the Department of Social and Family Affairs, Mr Tom Cavanagh, Atlantic Philanthropies (Ireland) Ltd, the Family Support Agency and Céifin itself. The outcome of this research became part of the 2008 conference

which posed the challenging question – 'Family Life Today – the Greatest Challenge?' The seed for that conference had been planted ten years earlier by a woman who asked me, almost in casual fashion, 'Who will rear the next generation?'

Community
What is it? How relevant is it? We began profiling a number of communities, underlining the local as a rich resource in its own right and stressing the importance of rediscovering connections.

Voluntary Participation in Community Activity
Without voluntarism, many services in Ireland would close down. Céifin promoted voluntarism wherever and whenever possible.

Spirituality and Values
Our society was searching for meaning. Modernisation was challenging engagement with Christianity and its values as irrelevant. Céifin began work on the idea of people taking responsibility for what it means to be Christian in practice.

Over the following decade, the Céifin annual conference continued to draw large attendances from a wide cross section of disciplines and age groups. They took place in Ennis, early in November, a time of year when delegates appreciated the opportunity to *recharge,* to power their lives with ideas and energise them for directions they may have forgotten or neglected. In the words of the poet Seán Ó Ríordáin, *'Ní cheadmhach neamhshuim'* – 'Indifference is not allowed'. One farmer memorably put it that 'Céifin fits nicely into the rhythm of my year.'

It was disappointing for me that so many of my confrères in the Killaloe diocese (with the notable exceptions of the bishop, Willie Walsh, and a few others) did not participate in the conferences and thus missed the opportunity to connect with debates that were really relevant to them. The media covered the conferences well, which helped to spread the message of the talks, many of which were prophetic in challenging the excesses of the Celtic Tiger era. A look at the conference titles over the years indicates the scope and depth of the issues that were tackled:

1999 Working Towards Balance
2000 Redefining Roles and Relationships
2001 Is the Future My Responsibility?
2002 Values and Ethics – Can I Make a Difference?
2003 Global Aspirations and the Reality of Change
2004 Imagining the Future
2005 Filling the Vacuum?
2006 Freedom – Licence or Liberty?
2007 Tracking the Tiger – A Decade of Change
2008 Family Life Today – The Greatest Revolution
2009 Who's in Charge? Towards a Leadership of Service

The conferences attracted speakers of the highest calibre from home – John Hume, Maureen Gaffney, Gearóid Ó Tuathaigh, Tom Collins, Fintan O'Toole, Willie Walsh, Richard Douthwaite (RIP), John O'Donoghue (RIP), Joe Lee, David McWilliams, Mary Redmond, John Lonergan, Jim Power, Paula Downey, Marie Murray, Cardinal Seán Brady, Nuala O'Loan, John Waters, Maurice Neligan (RIP), Paul Reynolds, David Quinn, Alice Leahy, Diarmuid Martin, Emily O'Reilly, Mícheál Ó Súilleabháin, Paul Tansey (RIP), Peter McVerry, Mary Davies, Mary McAleese and many more. From abroad there came an equally distinguished group of speakers – Charles Handy, Stephen Covey, Mike Cooley, Robert Putnam, John Abbott, Peter Russell and John Drew among others. Their papers were published annually by Veritas and collectively they represent a considerable bank of insight and analysis of our society in the new millennium. As always, of course, much of the value of these conferences was in the exchange of views informally over coffee, meal breaks and in late-night discussions! Each conference generated its own energy and delegates looked forward to the following year's issues. Céifin 1998–2009 was by no means a series of mere talk-shops. It represented connection, focus, influence and yes, inspiration.

Sadly the recession took its toll on Céifin and, in the absence of any further funding, the 2009 conference proved to be the last (for the moment!). If it was to be the last, then maybe its theme – 'Who's in Charge? Towards a Leadership of Service' – proved most appropriate. The question of leadership is surely one of the most critical issues facing us as a society today. There is a distrust of the institutions that were central to our lives in the twentieth century and, in the resulting vacuum, there is an ongoing search for the kind of leadership that will bring recovery and renewal. It is clear that a lot of organisations will have to return to first beginnings. What are banks for? What is the Church for? How do business and community connect? Is politics about parties or people? Where do young people turn?

At the 2009 conference, Paula Downey suggested that our wider social culture needs to be transformed by transforming the culture of the institutions that shape it. A headline in today's (12 September 2012) *Irish Times* reads – 'Leadership is the Final Ingredient'. It refers to an epic drawn All-Ireland hurling final between Kilkenny and Galway and in the accompanying article, Darragh Ó Sé wrote that the critical difference in a final can be a player showing the right sort of leadership at the right time. In this instance, it was Kilkenny's Henry Shefflin who almost single-handedly dragged his team back into a game they looked like losing. In the midst of all the frustration and anger our society is venting towards institutions that have failed them abysmally, Céifin believes that now is the time to dig deep at local level and nationally in the search for a visionary, participative and accountable style of leadership, a la Henry Shefflin on the hurling pitch.

We have inherited top-down, centralised command-control models of leadership, which only foster disconnection between leaders and those being led. Questioning and dissent are not tolerated and the protection of the institution is primary. Creativity and ingenuity are stifled. Passivity is promoted and a culture of dependence is created. Such leadership has now to give way to sharing power and authority and giving people a stake in the decisions that affect their lives. This kind of leadership is most obviously needed at local level in the Church and where it is exercised it releases a whole new kind of energy.

The new leadership will also have to be value-based. Market values without the support and influence of more noble ideals lead only to self and sectional interests. More of the same approach of the past will certainly not bring renewal and recovery. In the words of Mahatma Gandhi, 'We must be the change we wish to see in the world.' At the centre of recovery must be a renewal of community.

Céifin is committed to nurturing family, the basic unit of community. With the support of LEADER, Céifin commissioned a research project on where family is now and how it can be practically supported. It is our hope that the quality of information arising from this project will help design and implement a model of community involvement which will support family life.

If circumstances permit, Céifin hopes to develop a programme based on research into five hundred and eighty families in seven communities of varying population size. This programme will be based on the axiom – 'Act locally, think globally'. It will provide case studies, capability building, feasibility studies and training. These will be targeted at making real progress towards a new Ireland with local leadership, powered by local responsibilities.

Conclusion

For over a decade, Céifin facilitated reflective conversation on an Ireland which was experiencing extraordinary change – change which was brought about by technology – in the main, communications technology. The values associated with this change are material values. It has become obvious that market values have assumed an importance in recent times that is beyond appropriate. Economic behaviour is only one kind of behaviour and economic activity represents only one facet of human existence. It does not take account of people's relationship needs – with one another in families and communities – and it does not distinguish between the sacred and the profane. How society is to be organised and how people ought to live their lives should not be decided on the basis of market values.

So the question Céifin posed in 1998 – 'Are We Forgetting Something?' – is a valid one and it must continue to be posed even louder as we struggle through a recession that is putting serious pressure on individuals, families and communities. The recent Céifin study on family life clearly highlights the pressure that is weighing on families. Much of this pressure is coming from programmes and institutions over which people have no control and so they are looking back into their communities for solutions to their problems. This in turn is presenting communities and the clubs and organisations within them with enormous challenges. The outcome of the study also suggests that a rebuilding of trust – in the Church, in politics, in the banking system – is essential. This rebuilding can only be done on the basis of genuine response to people's needs.

One fact that was highlighted right through the Céifin conferences was that the twentieth century was very much concerned with the material. The twenty-first century would have to be about the spiritual, about looking deeply into what dehumanises people. The levels of substance abuse, crime, suicide, depression, fear and anger are reaching crisis proportions. In his book, *Beyond Prozac*, Terry Lynch says:

> According to the WHO [World Health Organization], depression will be the world's most pervasive serious illness by 2020. It currently affects 340 million people and represents one-third of psychiatric hospital admissions.

The solutions to these issues will not come from the same means that created the problems. Completely different approaches are called for and different kinds of systems, including a different kind of Church system. Otherwise the Church could be on the brink of losing at least two generations and we could face the prospect of an Ireland with no spiritual or ethical moorings.

As to Céifin's future, hopefully it will continue to pose those crucial questions, at least in the short term. It must also take the findings of the family study to a nationwide audience, make them available to every community, every agency, every sector of society. The challenge to institutions to facilitate the participation of people in all of this is vital and cannot be ignored by people in power any longer.

TWELVE

Values for Ireland

We felt it was important to pull together the key messages to emerge from the twelve Céifin conferences. The twelve spanned 1998 to 2009 with over eighty papers by national and international speakers who presented to a cumulative participation of approximately four thousand people, capturing substantial national attention. A friend of mine, Brian Callanan agreed to jointly work with me on this and we are currently seeking a publisher. So, *Values for Ireland* emerged. The title is a bit presumptuous. Our excuse is that the eighty speakers had put serious thought into their inputs and were as entitled as any other group to indicate our deep values for Ireland.

The conferences were futuristic, signalling many of the weaknesses embedded in the Celtic-Tiger approach with its reliance on property-led growth and short-term policies, resulting in the decline of community, the marginalising of human, social and spiritual values and overall becoming a debt-ridden society. The lessons from Céifin are that the path to recovery will not come from 'more of the same', i.e. values, style of leadership and institutions. The road to recovery will have to be based on radical change. We have grouped the messages from the conferences into four broad headings: Values-led Change, Social Capital, Resourcing People, and Power and Leadership.

Regarding *values*, the lessons from Céifin are that we need to focus on the twin values of our inner identity and collective potential drawing from both Christian and other traditions. There is an obvious need to integrate basic values into life – public and private.

Debate around values is important otherwise we lose the language. Economic or market values dominate debate. Social and soft issues to do with health, transport, schooling, etc. receive a fair amount of attention because they impinge directly on people's lives. However, many important issues are rarely dealt with and these are to do with relationships:

- With inner self;
- With others – family and community;
- With Creation – environment does receive some attention but nothing on the scale it deserves;
- With Creator – we believe we have become the generation with all the power and wisdom – in technology, economics, etc. – to the point of pushing God to the sidelines, and the wisdom of past generations to oblivion.

There is no doubt a modern economy requires a well-trained, well-educated workforce. Market and commercial values are central to economic and business development. However, when these values impinge on areas of life such as family and community or in areas such as health and law, the impact on society can have serious consequences. Events are now bringing home to us that our society cannot afford to ignore the fundamental causes for relationships breaking down.

Social capital is about connections between people, it is about community, co-operation and voluntarism. While Irish society is regarded as rich in social capital a more individualistic and impersonal lifestyle is beginning to emerge as we increasingly move away from face-to-face relationships with our neighbours and others in our community. Social capital is about caring for one another – in community and family but it is also about extending to other areas such as sense of place, pride in who we are and pride in *our* place. It also extends to policing, health, work and environment.

Resourcing people brings several challenges. If social capital is so important how are people resourced to connect? Resourcing people is vital in the context of a two-way pulling of our national roots – in one direction by steps towards regional and global government and in the other by demands of moving towards the local. We demand freedom but a crucial question is what to do with it when we get it. There is sufficient evidence to suggest that freedom can easily come to mean licence to do what we like.

One of the great challenges is to reflect on our inner selves, on the power of inner strength. We now have the opportunity to work on the reawakening of the inner dimension to our lives which for many has withered away. For people at work, there are critical issues: reduction of stress and realising the potential of employees. At school, in the family and community: helping people to think through things for themselves and encouraging creativity and imagination. For people in general, depression and stress have become serious issues. Facilitating a practical experience of the spiritual is crucial in helping people to cope.

In terms of *power and leadership*, there is an urgent need to facilitate participation in different areas of life – economic, social and religious. This can happen when we build the concept of leadership of service. Powerlessness corrupts by eroding the sense of personal responsibility that is central to any kind of ethical conduct. We know what happens when power is not held accountable. The key period in the development of contemporary Irish society was the period between the late 1980s and the early 1990s. It was in that period that the question of who would have power and who would not was essentially decided.

What is critical and tragic is that it was also the time at which the erosion of public ethics was at its most appalling and most vulgar. The loss of any sense of ethical restraint on the part of very significant sections of Irish society was at its strongest.

One of the great challenges now is to build the concept of leadership of service, focusing on truth, trust and integrity. The election of Pope Frances with his emphasis on this kind of leadership is significant and one for others in leadership positions to note.

THIRTEEN

Towards a Renewal of the Church

The late Václav Havel, former president of the Czech Republic, once spoke thus to the European Parliament:

> Today many things indicate that we are going through a transitional period, and it seems that something is on the way out and something else is trying to be born. It is as if something were crumbling, decaying and exhausting itself, while something else, still indistinct, were arising from the rubble.

Havel might well have been talking about the Catholic Church in the twenty-first century. We are in the transitional years, the cleansing years, the changing years. Transition is rarely without pain because it means letting go so that something new can be born. The letting go will be painful particularly for my generation of priests. We were formed in a different era, and in a different model of Church. We are older, fewer, and, to be honest, more tired now. As a Church, we are all suffering from a certain tiredness, a lot of engagement with ritual, habit, formality, and maybe too little engagement with Christianity. As priests engaged in renewal, our focus is perhaps too narrow. We look too much at ourselves. We want to create a Church renewed for ourselves, forgetting that the Church exists for the world. The *world* for most of us is local. It is the parish, the community, where people are at in their lives. It is the people we serve and what their realities are.

In John 3 we are told that 'God loved the world so much, he sent his Son.' That one sentence directs my life in so many ways. I heard that call fifty years ago as a student in Maynooth, when the world asked 'Church of Christ, what do you say of yourself?' The Church set out to respond to that question in *Gaudium et Spes,* a blueprint for a Church engaging with the world about which I have written earlier. It called us to be a Church where 'nothing genuinely human' would fail to echo in our hearts, a Church which 'travels the same road as all of humanity', attentive to the deep questions of the people of today, especially those who are troubled or poor or in any way afflicted (#1).

At the close of the Jubilee Year 2000, Pope John Paul II wrote a wonderful letter entitled *Novo Millennio Ineunte* – 'At the Beginning of a New Millennium'. He wrote:

> Let us go forward in hope. The new millennium is opening before the Church like a vast ocean upon which we shall venture, relying on the help of Christ.

He was inviting all of us to respond to the challenge of bringing the gospel of the twenty-first century to the world – to live our lives following the example and teaching of Jesus Christ. There are parallels with the very beginnings of the Church when, after a fruitless night's fishing, Jesus invited Peter and his companions to 'put out into the deep'. When they did 'they caught a great number of fish' (Lk 5). John Paul II invited us to 'put out into the deep' with a courage and a confidence based on the belief that Jesus would be with us always on the journey.

John Paul wasn't talking about some kind of new programme. It was much deeper than that. The programme already exists in the gospels and in the living tradition of the people of faith down through the centuries, centred on Christ 'who is to be known, loved and served'. He told us that the gospel has to be expressed anew in each generation so that it speaks now, to the issues people are living and the questions people have. It has to be 'translated into pastoral initiatives adapted to the circumstances of each community'. He asked each local church 'to set out pastoral initiatives', a pastoral plan suited to the local context because 'it is in the local churches that the specific details of the pastoral plan can be identified which will enable the proclamation of the gospel to reach people.' He asked us to be guided by three principles as we set about this task:

Holiness – knowing Jesus better and being more closely united with him. Everything rests on this.

A Spirituality of Community based on the belief that each one of us is made in the image and likeness of God. 'This makes me able to share the joys and sufferings of my brothers and sisters, to sense their desires and attend to their needs ... bearing each others' burdens and resisting the selfish temptations which provoke competition, careerism, distrust and jealousy.'

Compassionate Action on Behalf of Those in Need – 'I was hungry and you gave me to eat ...'

Finally, John Paul wanted us to be patient in deciding on pastoral initiatives, not to rush into things, but rather to 'be rooted in contemplation and prayer'.

In 2002, the diocese of Killaloe attempted to respond to John Paul II's call to 'translate' the gospel into 'pastoral initiatives' for our local context by developing a pastoral plan. For eighteen months a group of priests, religious and lay people, led by our bishop Willie Walsh (it is crucial to have the bishop at the heart of this process), worked on a process towards the development of a pastoral plan for our diocese. I was asked to be the director of the process and of the group which came together.

Often it is the questions we have which shape how we see things. I vividly remember the question that came to me at a meeting of the priests of the diocese at the beginning of our planning process. As they talked about the future of the Church, I found myself asking 'what is the Church for?' I realised that this crucial question shapes the kind of Church we become. Are we a devotional Church focused more on the next world than this one or an engaged Church in touch with the real lives of people *now*, called to be involved in the questions and the issues that people face today? A devotional Church sees its role as providing services for people to attend; an engaged Church seeks to serve people, where they find themselves, in all the different circumstances of their lives.

In the months that followed we set out on an extensive consultation process across the diocese, trying to listen to the real concerns of people and their hopes for the kind of parish and diocese we wanted to become in the years ahead. We tried to be as inclusive as possible, including people who had moved away from the Church. We received an extraordinary variety of viewpoints, comments and suggestions. There was a refreshing honesty to the conversations. This was healthy and good. Developments in education, communications, economics and cultural activities have given people a self-confidence that was lacking in the past. This self-confidence gave people a freedom to question systems and structures of authority and to take a more independent stand in relation to these structures. I had a sense of a local Church, priests and especially lay people, beginning to find its voice, beginning to ask questions and to look for accountability. Bishops, priests – or indeed anyone in authority – could no longer use authority without being accountable for its use.

Despite the wide range of viewpoints thrown up by our consultations, there were certain themes and issues which came up again and again. It was clear from the consultations that people were still open to the values and ideals preached by Christ, but the problem was connecting to the lived experience of people. Young people in particular said they experienced the Church as being distant and remote from their ordinary life concerns. Our rituals and faith language do not speak to them in ways that touch their lives. It was clear too from the consultation that many (though not all) priests saw it as a time of openness to new ideas. They have no desire to return to the rigidities and certainties of the past. Both priests and people spoke of the work of the Church locally in the previous century in terms of 'maintenance and management'. Masses were celebrated, sacraments administered, rules of morality spelled out for people, buildings constructed and maintained. All of this was largely done by the clergy. There was recognition among priests and people that this model of Church would not hold in the new millennium. It was too rigid and too distant from people. We need to move to a new model of Church.

FOURTEEN

A New Model of Church

Talk of a new model of Church might upset or frighten people, but there is nothing to fear. A model means the way the Church structures itself, the way it gives expression to what it is about and embodies who it is in society and the values it wants to live out. Our consultation across the diocese told us clearly that the old model, where bishops and priests were seen as managers and sole decision-makers and lay people as those who obeyed instructions, is well and truly outdated.

What model of Church can people resonate with today? Responding to what we had heard on the ground and listening to what God's Spirit was saying to us, we drew together a pastoral plan for our diocese, based on a new model of Church. This model saw partnership between priests and people as key to the Church of the future. In this model, reclaiming the significance of baptism is the starting point for each of us. Through our baptism, we have a shared dignity and equality among all of us – young and old, women and men, clergy and laity. That shared dignity implies a shared responsibility.

The parish is *our* parish. The diocese is *our* diocese. We do not *help* the parish. We *are* the parish. We *are* the Church. We are, as Pope Benedict would later say: 'co-responsible for the Church's being and action'.

Sadly, some baptised people do not feel they have a place in our Church. They feel excluded, sometimes because as they live their lives they may be in conflict with some aspect of the Church's moral teaching, or because they may be in conflict with some hurtful experience in the past with a priest or other Church person. There were no exclusions with Jesus. He welcomes everyone without exception. If our Church in Killaloe is trying to know, love and imitate Christ, it needs to be a welcoming Church, a loving Church, a listening Church and a humble Church, aware that always we are a community of saints and sinners, as it was in the time of Jesus. We wanted to live a vision of Church where everyone was welcome and could feel at home.

In living out this vision and trying to make it real in parishes, our pastoral planning group identified three general areas where the energies of the diocese ought to be focused in the coming years:

Prayer and Spirituality

One of the most frequent messages we received during our consultations was the absolute need to improve the quality of our Sunday Eucharist celebration. Among the factors which affect that quality are the priest's own faith, the relevance of the homily and too many poorly-attended Masses, rather than one real community celebration. How does my homily connect to a mother who has bundled her children into a car and made an effort to come to Mass. Will my words nourish her faith or theirs?

Our planning group proposed that a liturgy group be set up in every parish and that training and education be made available to them in order to develop more participative and better quality liturgies. These local liturgy groups would encourage and enable local creativity and talent. In the years which have followed, I have often been amazed by the creativity that can be harnessed in local communities, especially among women. One of the signs of hope in our Church is the number of small liturgy groups, mostly it must be admitted comprised of women, who support and sustain the celebration of liturgy in our parishes. We see the fruit of their work on big occasions, like Christmas and Easter but also at annual parish celebrations of harvest, and keeping memory at November, liturgies praying for exam students or other special occasions that reach out to people at significant moments in their lives. People are crying out for ritual to make sense of their lives. These groups do tremendous work in trying to link an often archaic liturgy to people's lives.

Liturgy still offers the possibility of meeting people at very significant moments in their lives. We have a great point of contact here if we can utilise it. I see wedding and funeral liturgies as important not only for those directly involved but also because they draw in people with whom we may have no other form of contact.

Speaking words that connect with people is one of our most difficult tasks as priests. When I see the faces of those in front of me who are, I know, living such different life experiences I wonder how it's possible to speak in a way that connects with each of them. One of the ways I have found helpful is a very old practice of *Lectio Divina* or 'divine reading'. It has its roots in the third century. We gather on Monday mornings after Mass for these sessions. It requires us to meditate, pray and contemplate what the Scriptures might be saying to us. I find it influences the way I celebrate the Eucharist. In my daily Mass I always take a few moments to pose the question, 'What is being said to us now and how can we connect it to our daily lives?'

Formation and Support

If we are to move to a new model of Church then formation and support are crucial. Our planning team saw this as vital for specific groups of people.

PRIESTS

A new model of Church challenges us as priests to move towards a new kind of leadership – from 'authority leadership' to 'servant leadership'. Christ himself said 'The Son of Man has not come to serve but to be served.' This is enormously challenging. We have been formed in a model of Church where bishops and priests exercised considerable power. This has been eroded in recent years – something which I believe can be of significant benefit to us as Church. We were formed to be independent, to work on our own, to make decisions without reference to lay people. We cannot underestimate the formation and support that is needed if we are to move to a model of Church based on genuine partnership.

PARENTS OF YOUNG PEOPLE

For me this area is crucial. A survey carried out by CMAC (the former name for Accord) a number of years ago identified the mother as the greatest influence in shaping people's Christianity – not the bishop, or priest or anything that happens in the church building. We need to acknowledge where the most effective participation in Christian formation is taking place or has the potential, namely, the home – through parents or the school – through teachers. There is a huge challenge here. While many young parents remain committed to their faith and its practice, many others have drifted away from the Church. It is often when they experience the joy and wonder of new life in their own children that they become more aware of and open to the deeper mystery of life. For this reason, programmes involving parents in Baptism, First Communion and Confirmation are a high priority. These programmes will be supportive of the excellent work teachers do in schools and will hopefully be effective in revitalising the parents' own faith and practice.

Adults Generally

Adult Christians need an adult faith. We have been slow as a Church to offer people opportunities to deepen their faith and develop an adult spirituality. It is true that the strategies already mentioned (liturgy, prayer, formation for parents) contribute to the faith formation of those involved. Our planning team saw the need to encourage the development of spaces where people could reflect on their faith as adult Christians. In days gone by, lectures and talks to large audiences were important, but it is now recognised that the most effective adult learning comes from small groups, where people can reflect on and share their experiences in the light of faith.

Young People

So many young people feel disconnected from institutions generally – be it Church, State or even family. A new model of Church is not simply about getting people 'back to Mass'. It is about reconnection and does not lend itself to simple solutions. We must go to where young people are, learn their language and try to connect with them there. There are many initiatives doing excellent work with young people, often in isolation. We need to tap into those initiatives, draw energy from their best practice and hopefully co-ordinate them into a diocesan programme.

JUSTICE

While people need to hear how the gospel is good news for their lives, they also need to be challenged towards a gospel care for the marginalised. Our planning group proposed a 'Justice Group' who would

- Listen to the marginalised – refugees, travellers, asylum-seekers, the elderly, urban and rural poor;
- Help to identify and speak out on current issues and emerging needs in the area of justice;
- Inform and sensitise all of us regarding our obligations in the area of justice at all levels.

Looking back it is interesting to note that this was perhaps the area of the pastoral plan in which least progress was made. As local Church communities, we haven't yet made the link between working for justice and living the gospel. We are still too introverted, too caught up in our own structures and in a devotional Church and not at the service of the world around us, especially those most in need.

Structures and Communication

The implantation of any of the foregoing require structures to be put in place. A model of Church based on partnership and participation simply will not work without new structures. Our planning team placed great emphasis on the role of parish pastoral councils. These were new groups, unlike the parish council model which functioned largely to maintain Church property, finance and buildings. Pastoral councils were new structures where priest and people together would make decisions about the pastoral needs of the parish.

We were very clear about what kind of group a pastoral council is – a representative group of the parish community, reflective of the parish's diversity. Its role is to listen to what is happening in the parish, to be aware of the pastoral needs, to discern how best to respond, and to plan accordingly. To do this a council needs to gather the wisdom and views of the entire community. It should be guided by one simple question – 'where and how is God calling us?' It needs to find ways of communicating what it has discerned as the way forward to the entire community.

We were also clear about what a pastoral council is not – a replacement for the parish priest or a bunch of Holy Joes, Holy Marys or parish priests' pets! It is not a fundraising body or a glorified debating society. It's not a token group of lay people. Neither is it a life-commitment – an agreed timeframe for stepping down and finding new members should be the norm.

The development of pastoral councils was one area in which I felt the diocesan plan had a very significant impact and it gave me hope in the possibility of moving to a new model. A two-year programme was put in place to establish a PPC in every parish. A booklet called *Forward Together* was produced to help support and facilitate the establishment of these groups. In a survey carried out some three years later, forty-three of the fifty-eight parishes in the diocese responded, of those all said that a PPC was in operation in the parish. I'm not saying everything was perfect but certainly we were moving in the right direction.

Obviously, all the foregoing suggests the need for an effective communications network. Our planning group proposed a diocesan communications committee which would

- promote the use of communications technology – website, email, etc.;
- monitor parish newsletters with a view to improving their quality;
- advise on the use of local radio and television;
- explore the feasibility of producing a regular diocesan newsletter.

Implementing the Diocesan Plan

The planning group which drew up the diocesan plan was expanded to form a new diocesan pastoral council who would help implement the three areas that we had identified. Directing this work became a huge focus for me in the following years. As indicated above a lot of work was invested in developing pastoral councils but there were also initiatives in the areas of liturgy, and sacramental preparation programmes, in setting up a new diocesan pastoral council and in moving towards a more participative model of Church.

We anticipated that the journey would be slow. Moving towards 'a new model of Church' is a huge cultural change, one that will not be accomplished overnight. A real change of mindset in both clergy and laity will take time. The journey is an endless one. At times, I was filled with hope seeing little steps being taken – more participation of laity, seeing lay people finding their voice and experiencing the Church as *their* Church. At other times there was frustration at the reluctance to change an inculcated clerical culture among priests and a deeply-engrained dependency culture among lay people.

As time went on, I became conscious of the urgency of that change. Our plan was written at a time when the impact of the aging profile of priests and a future with far less priests to minister was not yet fully in view. The urgency of preparing for a different kind of Church where parish communities would continue to flourish with the involvement and support of lay people became increasingly evident to me. The question that will be asked in parishes in a few short years down the road will not be whether there is a priest in a parish but whether there is a Christian community in a parish – one that is led by lay people. There is, however, a great deal of reluctance to face up to this emerging reality. There is a sense of denial among many priests and laity, both in terms of the speed at which these changes are approaching and the severity of their effect. It is not uncommon – and perhaps even understandable – to hear priests say that the present system 'will see me out'. However, this is not an adequate response to the mission of spreading the gospel in our parishes. We need much greater imagination if we are to effectively meet these challenges.

One of the challenges will be to envisage and accept new forms of ministry. There are two broad concepts of lay participation as I see it. There is the voluntary commitment of the people of the parish to the building up of their own local Christian community. But increasingly, this volunteer commitment will need support of other 'professional' lay ministers who will take up roles in formation and pastoral planning and support. We need to financially plan for a future where lay people with the required skills and formation are enabled to take up these roles. I think the future will see clusters of parishes which are ministered to by teams comprising priests and lay pastoral workers who together support local parish-faith communities. We must have the vision to prepare now for that future.

Note: In this chapter, I acknowledge the work of the Killaloe Diocese Pastoral Planning Group – of which I was director – and I have freely quoted from their ultimate report, '*Killaloe Diocesan Pastoral Plan 2004*'.

FIFTEEN

The Priest and the Priesthood of the Future

My involvement in social, development and planning issues in the New Ireland through SFADCo and the RRO, took me 'outside the box' of parish where the majority of my priest colleagues were in ministry at the time. I was really happy to be involved in pastoral and spiritual ministry in the new parish in Shannon, 'keeping my hand in' as it were. During this time I got a lot of requests to take on retreats for diocesan priests, religious and parish groups as well as talks to various groups, conferences, and a certain amount of media work. (This work brought me to twenty-two dioceses in Ireland and even to Scotland and Wales.) It was very challenging work but I wanted to involve myself in relating the gospel to a changing Church and a changing Ireland.

For a three-year period I was President of the National Council of Priests of Ireland. We focused on the priesthood – person and priest. We tried to paint an honest picture of the challenges we faced as priests and the issues which the Church faced in the second half of the twentieth century.

During this time, I came to see that most of the pre-Vatican II experience of seminary in Maynooth was closer to the world of the monastery than to the world in which we were preparing to minister. My experience of being in a non-Church setting in a university in Cardiff taught me a lot. I remember thinking after the experience that the priest of the future must be a grounded person, emotionally and spiritually able to stand on his own feet, confident in what he believed and in his ability to communicate it in a language people understood. There would be no 'hiding behind the collar' in a world shaped by very different values.

Many of the priests I knew and admired were deeply human people, at home in their own humanity. But it is also true that our formation did not prepare us for a world we were to minister in, a world dominated by industrialisation, urbanisation and economics. There was even disagreement about whether we should be involved in these issues. During the 1970s and 1980s the polarisation that surfaced after the Council widened as priests came to differ among themselves as to their role and the role of the Church. Were we to confine ourselves to the borders of our parishes, to see our role primarily as leaders of worship and dispensers of the sacraments? Or were we called to be actively engaged in the world, in all aspects of human life? On occasion it would be put to me that what I was doing was not 'priestly work', and suggested that there was no spiritual dimension to it. I would argue the opposite. To challenge the world with

Christ's values demands a deep spiritual dimension. It also means being prepared to suffer, and moving out of the comfort zone. This is an essential part of the Christian way.

I sometimes struggled with the fact that I wasn't involved, full-time, in parish ministry. To be honest, deep down my struggle arose from the fact that I was born with and grew up with a fairly conservative nature. From early on however, I had become convinced that the Church would have to become involved in real dialogue within itself and with the world around it. This of course would require considerable honesty and courage. If we turned away from that challenge, the vision inspired by the Second Vatican Council, one of engagement with the world around us, would be seriously threatened.

The post-Conciliar Church called for a different way of being Church and a different way of being a priest. Unfortunately, a lot of the promise was not fulfilled. And so the question: is it too late? Of course it is not but the Church must face the real challenges:

- understanding the world;
- understanding how to speak the Christian message today;
- a new understanding of leadership for our time;
- genuinely trusting the people of God;
- and a new understanding of what it means to be a priest.

Recently, a newly-ordained bishop called for a big drive for new vocations as the key to renewal of the Church. I wondered what model of priesthood he had in mind. At the time I had been reading a book by Richard Rohr, *Falling Upward,* which made me think about what kind of applicant who is considering priesthood today, and about promoters of vocations to the priesthood and the kind of priesthood they are promoting. Are they taking cultural changes into account, for example? I also wondered about the kind of formation that students for priesthood now undertake and if it will help them relate to and respond to the needs of people in the world of today.

Fr Rohr, a Franciscan Priest, author of more than twenty books and an internationally-known speaker writes about

> a generation of seminarians and young clergy who are cognitively rigid (lacking imagination) and 'risk adverse', who want to circle the wagons around their imagined secure and superior group; who seem preoccupied with clothing, titles, perks, and externals of religion, and frankly have little use for the world beyond their own control or explanation … Ecumenism, interfaith dialogue, and social justice are dead issues for them. None of us can dialogue with others until we can calmly and confidently hold our own identity.

If we are honest, we are all aware of the kind of candidate and model of priesthood which Richard Rohr has in mind. It is a cultic model of priesthood. It is evident that an increasing number of younger priests are attracted to this way of being priest. This will create real problems down the road. Younger priests conditioned by a cultic model of priesthood will increasingly be out of touch with priests from other generations in their dioceses and also significantly with lay people and the kind of Church to which they aspire.

We are very aware of the shortage of priests these days and we have few studying for the priesthood. But shortage relative to what? I sometimes think that we need to examine what we mean when we talk about this shortage. The reality is that much of the work undertaken by priests today could be done by lay people. Are there not lay people who can look after administration, finance, liturgy, as well as and much better than the priest? But if priesthood is defined in terms of responding to the real needs of people then we can speak of a shortage. These pastoral needs are everywhere. We need to be clear about the pastoral role of the priest, as one who nurtures faith by connecting with people in a meaningful way, in the experiences of their lives. This is the critical function of the person who is priest. We need a clear vision of this role in order to restore a clearer identity and affirmation for the priest.

The crisis we are living through is not just of *priesthood* but of *faith*. Faith itself is linked to the culture, the way of life of a people. My faith is rooted in the village I was reared in – faith permeated all of life there. The enormous changes we have described elsewhere have had a huge impact on people's faith. The question posed to me by George Thomason in Cardiff University: 'How is the Church going to cope with the New Ireland?' was very relevant but not addressed. Perhaps the leaders of the Church believed that the faith of the people would be unshaken and that the clerical model of power and control would continue as before. We live in a world where the kind of unquestioning faith we grew up with and the acceptance of clerical control are no longer tenable. People's faith in the Church and the priesthood has been shattered.

Where now will the children and young parents find their religious and spiritual roots? People connect through experiences. Jesus healed the sick. He listened to the marginalised, whether it was Mary Magdalene, or the Woman at the Well, and He fed the Hungry. He connected with the hearts of people and touched their souls. Following that example must be important for the pastoral mission of the Church at this time.

Only a Christianity which connects with people in language, stories, symbols that make sense, has any meaning today. Faith is nurtured in the simple day-to-day contact with people in coping with life. Faith can be restored only through experiences, through the lives of people being touched in a meaningful way. This is the role of the priest.

Faith is also fostered in developing ministries which give people an identity. The area gatherings in our parish have taught us the importance of a ministry which connects people to one another and to local area. The concept of a parish as a community of communities makes sense. We must discover Him in ways that make sense. There is an old saying, 'The person enriches the parish and the parish enriches the person.' The individual belongs to a network of relationships – family, friends, neighbours, and they exist in relation to community.

For example, I am writing this piece at the end of April 2013. On Monday evening of this week about thirty of us – men and women – met on the side of a hill preparing for our area gathering on May Eve. Its our twenty-first gathering in all. A number of farmers were part of this group and so we talked about the fodder crisis which has become a major problem for them and their animals. The conversation brought home to me the importance of sharing the burden. The following Thursday we met with the authorities of Shannon Airport as a result of which they agreed to make three thousand bales of silage available to farmers at a time when cattle were starving because of the shortage.

On Tuesday evening of this week a group of us – fifteen in all – many of them unemployed, met to discuss the possibility of establishing an initiative which would help people to cope. On Wednesday evening of the same week another group met regarding a bereavement initiative. At these meetings, grieving people and unemployed people, underlined how lonely and isolated they can be without support. If a local Church or Christian community isn't there for them in a structured way in these human experiences of loss and pain, then its sacramental life won't connect either.

These are all initiatives responding to particular needs at a particular time. We believe this is the way forward – beginning with the needs of people, especially those who are marginalised, responding to these needs as a local Christian Community but without using Church language.

A number of people involved in these are not churchgoers. I mention these because they point to the fact that the concrete, practical involvement is of major importance to the Christian Community. The reality is the Church cannot be fully understood without referring to the world. That world for most people is at local parish level.

In short, the mission of the Church includes the proclamation of the Good News of Jesus. The Church does this in the celebration of the Eucharist and the Sacraments, in His Word but it comes alive through experiences which are meaningful and which giving practical witness to the work of Christ in the reality of people's lives. The priest has a special role in all of this. So have the people.

Above all the person of Christ, His Word and His Presence in the Eucharist are at the centre of this way of ministering. The more we connect with the centre, with Him, the better we will connect with people. Connecting in our time will have to involve a deep encounter with the Lord. A contemplative Church, priesthood, and people is called for at this time. It is worth quoting Karl Rahner in this. He said 'People will be either mystics or unbelievers.'

Francis is certainly impressing people since he became Pope. He has repeatedly referred to a Church, a priesthood and to a Christianity that has to touch the lives of people and shape their environment. He has told priests they must not confine themselves to the sanctuary of their churches and has warned them of hypocrisy when they confine themselves to words but no action. He said:

> We have to avoid the spiritual sickness of a Church that is wrapped up in its own world: when a Church becomes like this, it grows sick.

In his addresses and gestures so far he seems to be a breath of fresh air. In a short time he has become an inspiration to people who love the Church but had seen it slip more and more into conflicts of its world and its own ends and away from the world it was founded to serve.

Francis has pledged to defend the marginalised and the poor and has called on priests to 'not grow weary of people's requests and needs, no matter how inconvenient, purely material or downright banal such appeals may seem.' (Pope Francis, Mass of the Chrism, 2013) I personally have been very uplifted by some of the things Pope Francis has been saying. I believe he could be pointing to a new direction for Church and priesthood which may bring us back towards involvement in a world 'God loved so much he sent his only Son.' (Jn 3:16)

Francis has challenged us with questions such as: Are we capable of bringing the Word of God into the environment in which we live? Do we know how to speak of Christ, of what Christ represents for us, in our families, among the people who form part of our daily lives? He speaks with simplicity and he calls on us to do the same. The Word of God that does not connect with the ground stays in mid-air. And to us priests he says: 'we cannot feed God's flock unless we let ourselves be carried by God's will even where we would rather not go …'

It seems to me this man is opening doors, inviting us to go out again and move into the world rather than away from it. This could mean a different mind is needed for many leaders in our Church with regard to what 'vocation' really means and with regard to formation for priests and people.

SIXTEEN

THE PARISH

The parish of Sixmilebridge and Kilmurry has a population of approximately six thousand. It is roughly equidistant between Limerick City, Shannon and Ennis. After Ennis and Shannon it is the third-largest population settlement in Co. Clare and is regarded as one of the fastest-growing villages in Munster. Between 2006 and 2011 it experienced a population increase of 51%. The enrolment at Sixmilebridge Primary School has almost doubled in the last decade. The parish has twenty-three housing estates, mostly occupied by young families.

When I came to Sixmilebridge as parish priest in 2006, a local doctor told me that 'Sixmilebridge people are homesters,' i.e. there was always employment to be found in the village or nearby. Long before most of the rest of the county was industrialised, Sixmilebridge had a reputation as a source of employment. By the beginning of the eighteenth century, the area had established a reputation for milling. At one stage seven mills had grown up around the village which grew around a crossing-place on the O'Garney river. Some of these had ceased trading by the mid-nineteenth century but the Thomond Woollen Mills, on the site of one of the old mills, still holds very fond memories for many of the present generation.

Around 1870 James O'Flynn came from a woollen-milling background in Newport, Co. Tipperary to set up the Thomond Mills. The mills flourished particularly with the outbreak of the Great War (1914–18) when there was demand for tweed, blankets and khaki. When the rest of the country was on its knees economically in the 1930s the Thomond Mills continued to expand, employing about ninety people. The workforce grew to one hundred and fifty in subsequent decades, due to the ingenuity of James O'Flynn in finding new markets in Europe and North America. The mill eventually closed in 1968 and the buildings were sold in 1970 to Clare Yarns.

When Clare Yarns closed, a number of smaller industries were developed. Many highly-skilled workers from the village also found employment with Lana Knit, a major textile industry in Shannon in the 1960s. Shannon Airport and Industrial Estate also provided employment for workers from the village. Brendan O'Regan, a Sixmilebridge man, became an internationally-recognised leader in the fields of industrial, airport and tourism development and was also a significant contributor to peace and reconciliation in a divided society. The school-going population of Sixmilebridge in the 1930s, 1940s and 1950s didn't therefore have to consider emigration nor even third-level education (which was only available to the few) – employment was on their doorstep.

Sixmilebridge and Kilmurry is a parish with a rich heritage, located in the foothills of East Clare with the O'Garney river running through it. It has a hinterland of good farming land, a wise farming sector and an industrious community which oversees a range of sporting organisations and voluntary services. With the encouragement of a very active Tidy Towns committee, local people take great pride in their place. The local railway station is crucial to the easy movement of people and goods. I came to minister in Sixmilebridge seven years ago and I have loved every minute of my time there.

My predecessor, Fr Pat Cotter, had laid the groundwork for the needs of an expanding young population. In 2004 the church was renovated as a place both of worship and of offering services to parishioners, particularly in the light of dwindling clergy numbers. A well-equipped parish office was built and Puff (we know her by no other name!) O'Connor was appointed parish secretary. Puff not only provides a professional approach to administration but she and her husband Christy have a deep love for the church. When I came to the parish, Jimmy Corry had been sacristan for nearly four decades – a legendary figure with an incredible knowledge of the place, its story and its people. When he died suddenly, we were bereft of the man and the service he provided, but fortunately Puff stepped into the breach to fill both roles – secretary and sacristan, with Christy as a powerful backup.

The parish office beside the church is centrally-situated and at times resembles an airport with people coming and going. It is where I can meet people, but more importantly it frees me up to concentrate on the pastoral and spiritual needs of parishioners, and especially to visit them in their homes. The provision of services which can be managed by a layperson much better equipped to provide them than I, is vital. There are also parish structures in place which facilitate the involvement of laity who take responsibility for decisions and action concerned with pastoral and parish activities.

The parish pastoral council was set up in 2009. This is a parish leadership team who in a spirit of partnership exercise the overall care and responsibility for the well-being and future of the parish community (see 'A New Model of Church' for more on this). Members are invited to participate and nominated by the parish community. They meet eight times a year and their term of office is for a maximum of three years, with the right to go forward for another three. The council has a central role in making and implementing parish decisions, while encouraging the active participation of all parishioners in the life of the parish community. An annual attractively-designed newsletter – *The Bridge* – keeps the locals informed on the many developments within the community each year, e.g. liturgy groups, focus on schools, Third-World links, parish finances and area gatherings. In order to respond to particular needs, the parish pastoral council established a number of subcommittees, e.g. on liturgy, maintenance of parish properties, youth ministry, bereavement, etc. One of the most active and successful of these subcommittees is the 'meaning to life group'. In what follows Annette Shanahan gives us an overview of the group's work since its commencement in 2007:

> From the beginning, through meetings and discussions, we identified the needs of our community and set out to organise gatherings to help us address the issues which challenge teenagers, parents, families – all members of our parish community. Our belief was that our church was more than formal ceremonies, more than fulfilling a duty, more than box-ticking. Our relationship with God was only as good as our relationship with each other, our lived faith. An action list of events evolved – an eclectic range of events, aimed at appealing to all of our community. One of the most successful was the 'area gathering', where we gathered as a community in different locations for Mass, music, dancing, reflection, food, tea and chat.
>
> We began a programme of events in 2007 which we hoped would feed the hunger for meaning in our lives. We had a very special evening with Liam Lawton, whose beautiful uplifting music touched our emotions deeply. Sr Stanislaus Kennedy spoke movingly of her work with the homeless and about the sanctuary she

has created in Dublin for reflection and healing. Her wisdom and unselfish devotion to her work nourished us all greatly. Our great soccer hero, Packie Bonner, was a big attraction who brought out the sports fans, young and old. He told wonderful tales of his soccer career and also of the roles of prayer and spirituality in his life. A true gentleman who spoke genuinely about his belief in God and his wish for all religious divides to be healed. Healing was indeed the theme for an evening with Fr Michael Collins – healing our rifts with God and with each other. We sensed the power of forgiveness, of letting go of old hurts.

For 2008 we decided to focus on parenting issues, in particular the parenting of teenagers. Clinical psychologist and broadcaster Dr David Coleman drew a full house of mainly young parents, many of whom might not be regular churchgoers. Issues of communication, respect and self-esteem were presented in a challenging way and the evening confirmed our resolve to continue with our parenting theme. Dr John Yzaguirre and his wife Claire had impressed many when they spoke at the Céifin conference about their 'Raising Caring Children' project in the USA. We invited them to Sixmilebridge where they shared their wisdom and insights with us on the skills and strategies that are needed to raise children who are emotionally healthy and socially competent. We progressed the parenting theme with a thoughtful presentation from Dr Patrick Ryan from the University of Limerick. He addressed the physiological changes experienced by teenagers as they progress and grow through the upheaval of adolescence. Finally, Nessa Breen, counsellor and mother, addressed the topic of 'Family Spirituality in Our Time'. She spoke honestly and helpfully about staying connected with our children, influencing their lives positively and trying to keep them connected with their faith in the midst of unfolding scandals within the Church.

In 2009 Conleth O'Sullivan led a six-week Life Skills programme which explored the participants' level of satisfaction with their lives. The desire for contentment is within all of us and it demands 'self-care' in order to ensure we are enriched and have the resources to be there for others, those we work with, live with and love. Meanwhile our 'area gathering' went from strength to strength and gave witness to the resourcefulness and enthusiasm of parishioners when the gathering came to their particular area.

Our programme for 2010 began with two personal and very powerful presentations on 'Recovering from Addiction' from Billy Fox and Gerry Roche. Billy and Gerry opened up their lives to a large audience and spoke with honesty and candour of their own personal journeys through addiction to ultimate recovery, and of the value of spirituality in that growth process. Fr Michael Rogers came to us from the Tearmann Centre in Glendalough to speak on 'Spirituality in Our Lives'. He drew us in the quiet of a candlelit church to treasure our sacred spaces, to embrace the here and now, to be open and available to each other, to respect our environment and care for our world. Spirituality is about co-operating wholeheartedly with God in bringing to fulfilment in our lives His design and plan for all life. One of the most memorable evenings for the parish was the visit of the Celtic Tenors. A terrific evening which lifted the spirit and nourished the soul. No one in the capacity audience wanted to leave, such was the invigoration the Tenors brought with their performance. We talked about it and remembered it long after we finally let them go! In the summer of 2010 we had a *Youth Activity Day*, when we brought a group of young people to the University of Limerick to learn about the Access programme and to participate in a range of activities.

Over the year 2011 we went through a period of reflection and tried to establish our vision for the Church in our parish. How might we enrich lay activity and ultimately the Christian community? How might we build social capital and foster leadership in the community? The closing of the local mart was a major landmark for the village and posed a challenge to us as a community.

Bishop Donal Murray opened our programme for 2012 with a scholarly and inspiring presentation on 'What does it mean to be a Christian?' 'Love one another as I have loved you' is a very simple rule but also a very demanding one. We need to foster in ourselves and others a contemplative outlook, to see life in its deeper meaning, as pure gift, in its beauty and its invitation to freedom and responsibility. Ultimately we discover in all things the reflection of the Creator and see in every person His living image. In a very practical presentation, Noreen Lynch, a pastoral worker from

Limerick, explored 'How we can better prepare ourselves and our children to connect to the power of God.' Spirituality has to be practised. None of us has all the answers on how best to live as family or community, but Noreen set forth some 'tried and tested' methods of coming together in prayer.

For our Lenten talks of 2012, Brian McMahon spoke on 'What the spiritual life means to me, personally'. Brian addressed the big questions – What is the purpose of life? Where am I going? Is there an eternity? What is it? He reflected on the many and varied ways the Holy Spirit works in our lives and he emphasised the power of prayer, scriptural reading and the sacraments. It was a very personal testimony in which Brian drew on the people who influence his life, from his father to his friends in the pub.

'A Soul for Ireland' was the theme of Bishop Willie Walsh's presentation. Bishop Willie has always challenged us and is never afraid to challenge the Church as an institution. The Church has become too introspective, he argued, too obsessed with self and personal holiness. Holiness needs to be alive in our communities in a meaningful way, as a real presence like Christ among us. We need to search for a 'a soul for Ireland', to seek renewal of values and principles to guide us in our lives so we can appreciate where we have come from, where we are now and where we might move to from here. We must be hopeful, be willing to debate and seek values to shape our lives. Those in leadership must vacate their seats at the table of privilege and stand at the altar of principle…

I am grateful to Annette for her comprehensive overview of the work of the 'Meaning of Life' Group. I included it here to give an indication of how vibrant this new model of Church can become – a community journeying actively together in faith, hope and love. Connecting with the real needs of people, bringing the gospel message into our real world and encouraging and affirming local initiatives and people, is what we as a parish community do. I am proud of our parish's efforts in that regard and with gratitude I continue to journey with them.

SEVENTEEN

A Day in the Life

24 May 2012. Yesterday was a busy enough day, but not in any way unusual. I am always amused when people come up to me at Christmas or Easter and say 'God, you are fierce busy these days, Father.' I tell them these are for me the easiest times of the year. People assume I am busy when they see me on the altar a lot – for Mass or a wedding or a funeral ceremony. Most of my work is done quietly or behind doors.

We don't have a funeral every day, but yesterday we laid Johnny Casey to rest. Johnny had suffered a heart attack on Sunday. He was the fourth brother in his family to die at a relatively young age. I realised the impact this would have on his remaining siblings, so I spent a lot of time with them, talking with them, listening to them, organising the funeral – just *journeying* with them. At the funeral I posed the question – what does Johnny's life teach us? Two things.

1. Johnny was a stonemason. Never out of work all his life. He had the gift of hands and always knew where he was going in life. Contrast that with so many young people today who are caught up in an

academic points race to get to college. And then what? So many of them don't know.

2. Johnny had the gift of time. He was never in a hurry, had loads of time for everyone – and yet the work was always done.

After the funeral, I called to see a young woman who lost her husband a year previously. When she opened the door to me, her eyes filled with tears. The first anniversary is a difficult time. It is memory time. What were we doing this time last year? This week is a much more difficult week for her than the week of the funeral, when family and community were there to support her. So we chatted and struggled and I listened to her spiritual and emotional needs. It was difficult.

From there I called to a forty-year-old man who, in the week he had buried his father, was told he had cancer. He had been through a severe bout of chemotherapy. Having experienced cancer myself in the past year, I could empathise with him. He told me that talking had been helpful to him. When physical suffering comes, it is important to stay mentally strong and tap into the energy coming from the people who are praying for us.

Later in the day I called to see a young couple who had asked to see me. Their teenage son has had major surgery on his back and is returning to school to prepare for his Junior Certificate examination. As a family they have been through a lot and they just wanted to talk. From there I called to two hospitals to see two older parishioners. (Once a month I visit the housebound, approximately thirty.) It is so important to give them time. That is all they crave. A quick 'hello – I'm praying for you – goodbye' from the doorway is not enough. Then last night we had a meeting of a small group who are setting up a Bethany Bereavement support group in the parish. We want to get it right, so we are taking things slowly. It was a busy day, but not an unusual one.

When the late John O'Donohue published his first book *Anam Chara,* he rang to ask what I thought of it? I told him it was very powerful, but there was one thing missing. 'What is that?' he enquired. 'It's the hill. The cross,' I replied. 'You're right,' he said. 'The cross will be in the next book.' All those people I met yesterday are carrying the cross.

When I was a student in Maynooth, we were advised to avoid the world of emotion. Our theology was too rational, too cold, too analytical. It was too much about the head and not enough about the heart. In the past the Church has emphasised ritual in the form of public and private prayer – and rightly so – but the way forward now is surely to go deeper into the contemplative dimension of spirituality, to let the word of God into us, to let the light of Christ into our lives. I see many people moving toward contemplative practices in the shape of yoga, Buddhism, etc. This is fine but a lot of those practices are comfort practices only. Christian spirituality has another dimension – the cross. The contemplative dimension needs to be brought back into dialogue with the theology of Christianity. But it has to be engaged contemplation. In the book *Faith Maps* (ten great twentieth-century thinkers), the Lutheran theologian Dorothy Soelle has written powerfully about this. Without the dimension of justice, she claims, and 'the theology of mystical resistance', the picture of faith could become lopsidedly personal and spiritual. In other words, it could become the religion of the rich. 'Our Godtalk could remain insulated and removed from the wounded out there in the world,' Soelle claims.

We need to connect with the spiritual needs of people as they are living their lives. Hitherto our connection was very much pastoral. We talked the language of prayer, the language of formulae – but there is another dimension to the spiritual world – the contemplative dimension. We used to think of this as the preserve of closed orders, but now we come to realise how valuable these orders are to the world – witness the numbers visiting the Poor Clares for example. We need to bring that contemplative dimension out into the world.

We have neglected the Holy Spirit in Christianity. When Jesus ascended into heaven, the disciples lacked courage and were afraid of the outside world. But Jesus had said – I have to go but I will send the Holy Spirit, the spirit of truth. You have to face the truth. How relevant is that for today's world? We need the courage to go into the world and not be afraid of all it throws at us. Developing a contemplative spirituality is a major part of that.

In Maynooth we were encouraged to meditate, but as time went on, we became very busy focusing on the externals – saying Masses, officiating at ceremonies, praying, reading the breviary. For a lot of us, myself included, the world of meditation slipped away. If you don't nourish the contemplative dimension, how can you connect with others? You cannot give what you haven't got. The heart goes out of what we do. We need to connect with people in a language that they understand. We call ourselves a Christian community. By definition that has to be Christ-centred. We must give time to thinking about and reflecting on what Christ is saying to us. It is as important to break the Word as it is to break bread.

EIGHTEEN

THE GATHERING

In Sixmilebridge, we like to think that in some ways we anticipated the theme of the Fiftieth International Eucharistic Congress held in Dublin in June 2012 – 'The Eucharist: Communion with Christ and with One Another.' For five years we have been holding area gatherings during the summer on that very theme. Interesting too that the assembly before the final Congress Mass in Croke Park was referred to as 'the Gathering'.

The Church is a Eucharistic community. We gather around the altar. We come together to listen to the Word of God. We witness bread and wine become the body and blood of Christ. There is great privilege in partaking of this mystery. It is a huge gift that we can never take for granted. And we do this gathered as a community. I love the tone of the bell on Sunday morning. I have this romantic notion of it calling the people from the hills and the valleys into one building to share in the mystery of communion with Christ and with one another – people of every age and status, all equal before Christ. For me, the gathering is a big definition of community. When the vigil Mass was introduced on Saturday evenings, one of the Clare hurling team said to me – 'What did ye bring that in for? What had we on Sunday but the Mass and the Match?' He was making the point that the gathering on Sunday was about Mass, but it was also about community. The people gathered outside after Mass to chat about the match or other important local affairs.

When I went to Sixmilebridge as parish priest, I felt that while the church is a sacred space, the gathering needed to be taken out to the community as well. So, every summer for the past five years, beginning on May Eve, we have gatherings in different locations – a hillside farm, a lakeshore, the green on a housing estate, the mart, the crossroads, the cemetery, the railway station – bringing Christ's message to people where they live and work in their own communities. It has been an extraordinarily popular and beneficial concept which engages the particular community in its preparation and execution.

Early in the year the parish pastoral council initiates discussion on the venues for the gathering. Sites are identified and local volunteers mobilise support and drive the idea on from there. It reminds me of the Olympic flame – you bring the torch to an area, put the preparations in place and let the games begin! Preparation is all-important. If the venue is a farm, we don't go near it until the silage is cut. Local volunteers and the pastoral council visit every house in the area and invite people to the gathering. It is so important that people feel included. They are also invited to write the story of that locality – there may be familiar landmarks such as a Famine village, a holy well or an old schoolhouse. They trace the people who lived in the area and what they meant to the community – and also what these landmarks mean *now*. The pastoral council will publish the local history in leaflet form. It is all about feeling rooted and connected.

An altar is erected on the site and a very special Mass is celebrated. The liturgy focuses on the significance of the area chosen. The readings and the offertory gifts are connected with the place. The local people do the readings and supply the music. After Mass, as dusk gathers, a bonfire is lit. The tea and sandwiches appear, followed by dancing, music and song from local musicians. The celebration will go on into the small hours, with as many as five or six hundred people present. Later, a commemorative plaque will be erected on the site by proud locals and will thus become a landmark for visitors and future generations to reflect on the day 'the gathering' came to the area.

The weather never bothers us. The Lord and local initiative will always provide. We had arranged a gathering for Reilly's Hill when the heavens opened and thunder and lightning intervened. Pat Reilly had a Plan B however. He had his vast slatted house cleaned and ready and five hundred people thronged into a cattleshed for the Eucharist. As it happened, RTÉ filmed that event and we got a huge reaction from around the country. Some people suggested that this was a twenty-first-century version of the Station Mass of old. Another 'gathering' site was Teereen Lough, where the community assembled on 4 August 2010. A young local woman, Irene Fleming. subsequently wrote about the evening:

> We decided to allocate the roles of the Mass across as many houses in the townlands as possible to include the involvement of many individuals. All the gifts we chose for the offertory were of special local significance (Gloster Well water, a hurley, a Clare jersey, a fishing rod, a Munster Minor Championship Cup). During the celebration of the Eucharist we remembered those from whom we inherited our Christian tradition. Local farmers granted permission for their fields to be used as car parks. The amount of people who attended surpassed all our expectations. The chat, music and songs did not finish until the wee hours of the morning. Friends and neighbours witnessed something very special that night.
>
> The 'area gathering' was successful not only for the residents of Drom Abhalán, Cill Cornáin, Rath Lubhaidh and Sean Daingean, but also for those who gathered from the various corners of the parish. The spiritual needs of the people were met above and beyond what we imagined. Our collective gifts were harnessed for the good of the local community. To paraphrase Fr Harry, 'A little bit of heaven was present that night.' People ventured outside their comfort zone and came together in a new way. The old *meitheal*

system of neighbours helping each other has returned to twenty-first-century rural Kilmurry. The old seanfhocal *Is fusa cruinniú ná scaipeadh* ('A gathering is easier than a scattering') has applied to our community since that August night.

I am always conscious that the Celtic year revolved around four great feasts: 1 February, with the start of tilling, the birth of lambs and the return of fishermen to the sea; 1 May, when the cattle return to the grass; 1 August, the celebration of the first fruits of the harvest and 1 November, the feast of the disappearing sun and the closeness of the *Other World*. There was also the great mid-winter feast, now our Christmas, and one at mid-summer, which we celebrate as St John's Night. These great feasts were integrated into the lives of Irish Christians. They were part and parcel of life and living.

We have tried to revisit many of these feasts, especially the summer ones, through our 'area gatherings'. I feel that the Celtic world still speaks deeply to us. It spoke to our people for over two thousand years until a clerical Church purged many of the traditional practices and associated ritual celebrations. Yes, there were excesses (usually involving alcohol) associated with these celebrations but in purging them the Church lost connection with something very deep in us. We have tried to remember these traditions, in an effort to link faith and culture, but also because they have a profound connection to nature, to the cycle of the seasons with which our mechanised and technological world is very much out of touch. Reconnecting to the rhythm of nature, also reconnects us body, mind and spirit, and makes us aware of the hand of God in all that is around us. So we celebrate as much as possible out in the air, in the fields, close to the land, by a lake, with the animal world all around us. We also light the bonfire, as our ancestors did at certain times of the year, especially mid-summer. As darkness draws in on a summer's evening, the crackling fire lights up the night and we gather in for music and storytelling and song. Earth, air, fire and water. A people gathered. Food shared. Music and song. Surely God is in this place, among us.

So the area gatherings have gone from strength to strength. These occasions make a massive contribution to the development of community. They are not just 'something for the weekend'. The attendances are strong and young people are heavily involved. Someone said that the parish has become 'as adept as U2 roadies' at organising outdoor events with attendant choirs, musicians, dancers, copious trays of food and the old dependable Burco boiler.

I love the notion of celebrating *the local* in the townlands of the rural areas and in the twenty-three different housing developments in the parish of Sixmilebridge and Kilmurry. One of the comments I most frequently hear is that people feel a sense of belonging and connection on those nights. People become comfortable with their neighbours and their own place, especially those who are new to the area.

They get to know people, to learn something of the local story. Some people who attend the gatherings are not 'regulars' at our Sunday liturgies and are all the more welcome for that reason. There is so much talk today about 'getting people back to Church'. It has to happen the other way around. The Church must go out to people where they are and connect with them. The area gatherings help us to do that.

This year we celebrated our twenty-first area gathering. We assembled on a hill looking south-west to Kerry, north-west to Galway, east to Maghera. It was on Pat Meehan's farm. The preparations, as always, were huge and special. The people from around Kilmurry and surrounding areas got involved. Young people prepared the history, the story of a people and a past. Tools and implements from the past were gathered. They included a one-horse mowing machine, a *slean*, a churn. Symbols of our history such as a bucket of spring water, local fresh eggs, home-made butter were brought. The Mass itself reflected all these connections. It was May Eve and so we blessed the land, the animals – cattle, horse, ass, goats and hens. Afterwards there was food and tea for everyone and a cake which had to be specially cut to celebrate our 21st! Music, song and chat followed and Mike Glynn mesmerised us with his stories. We went deep into the dark of the night, enjoying one another's company. One man said to me, 'The young people are enjoying this, but so are we all, young, middle and not so young.'

The gatherings are no longer a novelty for the people of Sixmilebridge and Kilmurry parish. They run through each summer and instil true pride and communion in the different localities. Hopefully they will help each one of us to (quoting the motto of the closing Mass of the International Eucharistic Congress) 'become what you receive'.

NINETEEN

The Story of the Mart

In late November 2007 Golden Vale Marts made a shock announcement. After close on thirty-four years of business they were closing Sixmilebridge Mart. This shocked the local farming community. It hadn't been predicted by any commentators. The local IFA (Irish Farmers' Association) branch had their AGM the following week. It was proposed that the farmers would organise and ask Golden Vale to reconsider their decision and reopen the mart. I was approached to lead a delegation to meet with the CEO and management of GVM (Golden Vale Marts Auctioneering Firm) to demand that the mart remain open. The auctioneering agents stood firm. We were told that the mart would not reopen and furthermore it would not be sold to any person or group who intended opening it for mart business.

We had the difficult task of reporting back to the meeting. At this assembly a small committee was formed with the aims of performing a feasibility study to examine the situation of possible local funding. Shortly after this meeting, the mart was offered for public sale with a guide price of €450,000. In January 2010 the mart committee made an initial offer of €220,000 to mark an expression of interest in the mart on behalf of the community. Fundraising commenced over the following months and shares were priced at €500 each. From the outset, there was great local interest. From all over the surrounding area the people stood behind the efforts of the mart committee and wanted its retention in the community. Too many local services had been taken away down the years never again to return to the local community.

During the following months the local people were kept informed of progress at public meetings and also at the Masses at the weekends. The reopening of the mart had now become a movement. This lobby group was no longer confined to the parish of Sixmilebridge and Kilmurry alone but had gathered plenty of momentum spreading to neighbouring parishes too. Support (and share purchases!) came from people in Clonlara and Truagh, Broadford, Kilkishen and O'Callaghan's Mills, Meelick, Newmarket-on-Fergus, Tulla, Quin, Clooney and Maghera and Shannon to name a few. By March 2010 we were convinced this was a viable project. However, GVM was determined that the mart was not for sale for the purposes of a mart. Further meetings were held and many phone calls were made but little progress was made. This was frustrating for all involved.

In May 2010, the mart committee convened a decisive public meeting. Farmers, members of the parish council, people with business interests and individuals from the wider community attended. Those present were informed that huge interest was shown in response to the door to door, person to person, invitation to participate through the shareholding initiative. However GVM were not budging. They were insistent that under no circumstances would they allow the sale if the purchasers intended to continue to trade as a mart. That night frustration was high among some of those present. A number expressed disappointment at the lack of progress. They felt we were wasting our time, and proposed that we withdraw, giving back the funds to the shareholders. The annoyance of this group was very understandable. They were disheartened and felt that the auctioneers had set their stall and had no intention of ever changing their mind. Their anger and upset was palpable. The exercise could easily have come to an abrupt ending. We were at a crossroads in this campaign.

I felt the need to intervene. I did not want to see so much local effort come to nothing. We were in a predicament. We were up against an inflexible company who had their own reasons for closing the mart. However, I also saw that stopping now would have serious consequences. I outlined to those present, as best I could, the impact that standing down would have. I pointed out that this wasn't just a farmers' issue but affected the whole community. After so much effort and good will, stopping now would be very demoralising. People would feel disempowered and this would undermine our self-belief as a community. This was a time when the recession was impacting on people's lives. Our community hadn't escaped, it too was affected heavily. If we 'threw in the towel', if we gave-in to a big company decision to close the mart without resisting we would once again allow the 'big' to overpower the 'small'. In doing so we would have accepted the model that allows big companies to do as they wish, without reference to the needs or wishes of communities in which they operate. I also believed that this was also an issue of justice, that the people of Sixmilebridge had a right to have a say in a decision which would have such a big impact on their community.

As with all groups, the despondency of some people about the progress made can take hold and influence others. I felt it was important that the commitment to the project would be clear and so I asked the chairman to put the question to the floor: did those gathered want to continue with the campaign or stop? The decision to continue was overwhelming. It gave a new lease of life to the campaign. Between May and December we continued with further bids but most importantly we now had the determination to keep going. We had found new strength as a community and were more united than ever in trying to achieve our goal.

In October 2010 we increased the bid from €300,000 to €350,000. However, this time our offer had a stipulation. We sought a response from the GVM group within a month. The committee was no longer afraid to take a stand. It would have suited the vendors at this point if we had gone away, but by now there was huge local support behind the mart and there was no question of backing down. GVM did not reply to us within the timescale we had set, so in November we withdrew our offer. We felt we were left with no other option by GVM We then let them know in no uncertain terms that we were unhappy with how the negotiations were unfolding. At this stage our business baby teeth were well and truly cut. We were delegates with a mandate.

In December an auctioneer on behalf of GVM contacted me to ask us to reactivate our offer and a subsequent meeting was arranged with the GVM group. Three members of our committee (I and two others) attended a meeting with them and negotiated on behalf of the community. We once again offered our maximum bid of €300,000. This time we were successful, it was accepted and the sale was agreed. This was a great relief among all those involved after months of discussion, planning, briefing our shareholders and renegotiating. We had finally achieved our goal. After some further delays contracts were signed and a full shareholders meeting was convened for Tuesday evening, 28 June 2011. On that evening a Board of Directors was elected and a plan of action put in place. The agreed opening date was Saturday, 27 August 2011.

An enormous voluntary effort sprang into action lead by the chairman of the board, Pat O'Reilly. Pat had been a stalwart, totally committed from the inception of the idea and through the negotiations with the company. Many others contributed enormously to this campaign. A few deserve a special mention; Pat Enright, Stiofán Fitzpatrick, Brendan Considine, Paul O' Neill and John Lyons. There were numerous people who gave tireless commitment and encouragement. It would be impossible to name them all. Many of the people involved in the mart were themselves farmers but lots of others were not, Tom O'Dea (Chairman of the parish pastoral council), Jim Corbett, local residents, public representatives, men and women of all ages.

The mart was opened on 27 August as planned, under the new manager, Seán Ryan, and the new board. There followed the best ever trading period with capacity sales and record prices. From that day to this, the mart has continued to flourish. It has been a great success story for our community. The mart is a great source of employment, providing two full-time positions and twenty-three part-time posts. A country market was subsequently established where vendors can sell their local produce and other goods including, fish, fruit, fowl, fuel, hardware and pigs. This venture too has gone from strength to strength. It is said that success breeds success and this is evident in the spin-off industry thriving alongside the mart. The ripple effect is quite evident in the locality.

As well as being a great economic success the opening of the mart has big social implications. At a time when farmers feel isolated the mart acts as a social hub. Many of them meet very few people during their working week. The mart is a vital gathering place for the stories, the chat and the sharing of news. It is a place for people of all ages and of varied backgrounds and profiles to come together. The value of this cannot be overestimated at a time when isolation is a major problem in rural communities.

The story of the reopening of the mart in Sixmilebridge, a large village in South East Clare, is summarised by the old Irish saying *Ni neart go cur le cheile* – 'There is no strength without unity'. It's about the power of the people uniting to harness the power of community. It shows the power a community can generate when it comes together with a shared purpose and resolve. It is also about conviction, determination, patience, persistence and leadership.

The purchase of the mart from Golden Vale was the result of huge voluntary effort. Witnessing the fundraising, the site preparation and the renovation of the mart for reopening by farmers, non-farmers, neighbours and friends was inspiring. People who didn't even know each other got involved and worked side by side for the common good. It's an example of a community taking back from larger companies and corporations ownership of busy infrastructural assets in their own localities.

The mart in the Bridge has for many years been a place for the trading of livestock and economic activity. It is now a hub of satisfaction and pride for shareholders (all six hundred and fifty of them), the wider community, patrons and visitors alike. The mart story proves that the co-operative model is a viable one at a time when people have lost faith in larger institutions and corporations. The message is: 'Support and retain what is local but at the same time grow it with activity, creativity and vision.'

TWENTY

Our Own Resources

Milk is a natural and nutritious drink. We in Ireland are blessed to produce grass which in turn, through our dairy farms, produces this humble liquid which is vital for the economic and social life of the farming community. For previous generations life on the farm was largely organised around milking times and the demands of the cows. Milk production was a labour-intensive business for those generations. Milking was done by hand and then came the separation of the cream, the churning and the making of butter.

In 1894 Sir Horace Plunkett founded the Irish Agricultural Organisation Society to propagate the idea of co-operation as a principle in farming. The idea took off and co-operative creameries were born. The creamery movement was particularly strong in East Clare. Feakle was one of many villages to have a creamery, which had a huge social, as well as economic, significance. My memory of the village, as a youngster in the 1940s, is of a busy place as every morning horses and carts – and donkeys too – brought milk to the creamery and later returned home with the skim milk for the calves. The creamery itself was a great meeting place and a focal point for the news of the day – the scandals, the gossip, the weather and the state of turf, hay and hurling. The postman spent some time there as he could deliver mail and save himself several trips up and down the various boreens. The creamery cheque was a vital monthly income for the farmer, who would then support local businesses by shopping for the tea, sugar, flour, tobacco, etc. In my childhood over one hundred farmers supplied milk to Feakle creamery, which had a permanent manager and assistant.

'Fair' days were also days of social and economic significance. Bohan's public house would open at five o'clock on a fair day morning to cater for farmers arriving early with their cattle. And of course they would be in and out during the day as deals were – hopefully – done. Later, the mart served the same purposes – social and economic.

Feakle was a hive of industry in so many ways. On one short road (which we called 'the ould road') there lived a shoemaker, a chairmaker, two wheelwrights, three tailors, five gardaí, a doctor, a teacher, two priests and a number of shopkeepers. Music was also a major part of our lives and Paddy Canny was the master of the fiddle. He once told me he picked up the music by listening to his father teaching the fiddle to neighbours, while he (Paddy) was supposed to be doing his homework! The music was just a natural part of our lives. When I was a student in Maynooth I asked my father if I could get a tape recorder. He said I could – if I cut, saved and sold two tractor-loads of turf! I did, and my first venture with the recorder was into Paddy Canny's house. He played for four hours without ever repeating a tune. I was so privileged to know this humble and gifted man.

Overall, however, little enough effort was made to encourage and nurture the music and the musicians. It was only when *Radio Éireann* (largely in the person of Ciarán Mac Mathúna) brought that music onto a national stage that its importance outside ourselves was noted. Now, thanks to Seán Ó Riada, Micheál Ó Súilleabháin, the Chieftains and many others, Irish music is on the world stage.

Let me state clearly that all the foregoing is not intended as a wallowing in nostalgia and longing for days that are gone. The 'good old days' had plenty of 'bad old days' among them that no one would want to revisit. We have come a long way in improving living standards but maybe now is the time to pause and reflect on our values.

Farming as we know it is a relatively modern phenomenon. From the time our hunter-gatherer ancestors decided to stay put and work the soil to now is a relatively short step in history and for much of that time farming was of a static and subsistence nature. The Industrial Revolution brought machinery that would improve and extend the possibilities of agriculture. The growth of cities brought huge populations that had to be fed. Two world wars in the twentieth century brought further acute problems in the provision of food for the masses. Subsidies, science and technology, research and development were applied to what had been subsistence farming. This led to intensive farming, characterised by mass production which consumed large amounts of energy and concentrated on high-yield varieties needing high levels of pesticides, fertilisers and water. Animal-rearing became intensive and large-scale. In the space of four or five decades we have moved so far – to the point where we have basically solved the food production problem – but we strive for ever-higher yields and greater intensification. This puts greater strain on the land and on nature generally and calls into question our ultimate values and our connection with the land.

The rural environment has also changed dramatically over the same period. Urban sprawl, industrialisation, afforestation, the growth of tourism and recreation, the construction of road networks and other infrastructural developments – all of these have intruded on the rural landscape. That landscape has been shaped over millennia by slow interaction between nature and man – at a pace which allowed nature to adapt and adjust. That pace has quickened noticeably in recent decades. If we begin to abuse the landscape and all that live on it, seeing it only in economic terms, it is a short step to abusing our fellow humans and ultimately damaging our relationship with the Creator.

The landscape is not merely the place where food is produced. For most of those who farm it, it is home, but it is also home for an increasing number who do not farm or who farm part-time or are engaged in off-farm work or alternative enterprises. It is the place where many retreat, even escape, from the intensity and stress of urban life. At a deeper level, the countryside is where our roots are, where we really belong.

So the question I am asking is have we disconnected from the land – and at what cost? It is at the very least time to pause and reflect. Are there other ways of connecting with the land – ways that are more sustainable of the environment, of the human community and of the human spirit? Our fathers and forefathers nurtured the land, respected it, cared for it. You could see it in the way they opened a drill for potatoes. They never forced the land. We need to rediscover the connection they had with the land. A small but growing number of people argue the need to move towards a transformation of the current food system into an 'organic and beyond' future.

The human spirit needs connections in order to balance the needs of the body. One of these connections is with nature. The rural landscape has a spiritual, as well as an economic, value. That landscape has to be understood for its cultural value in all its forms – not just its valleys, hills, rivers and lakes and all that live on them, but its music and story, its lore and legend too.

The question keeps recurring to me – does the past have a future?

TWENTY-ONE

Does the Past have a Future?

Yesterday I got a telephone call from a man who wanted me to visit his wife who was quite ill. That man was Paddy Donoghue, the last living member of the original Tulla Céili Band, founded in 1936. When I made the visit to his wife, I got talking to Paddy. I suggested to him that there was a time when people like him would almost be ashamed to take down a fiddle and play. It would be associated too much with the repressed past. Nowadays with people like Martin Hayes, traditional music is very big on the world stage. In our search for identity, areas of life like music, dance and language, have taken on a new lease of life.

There never was a more important time to consider the concept of community and our immediate *local* world. For years we worried about Dublin being the centre of power, but then much of that power went beyond that to Brussels and to the whole global influence. One of our greatest challenges today is how the local will respond to European and global influences. Years ago I reckoned that Ireland consisted of about two thousand communities (don't ask me how!). They were of various shapes and sizes. Central to each one of them were the two pillars of sport and Church. Mostly, the GAA defined the parish and the parish defined the Church. Today those communities are changing out of face. Some are expanding at a phenomenal rate with the advent of vast housing estates.

In the west of Ireland, contraction is the word, with parishes often clustering to provide a team in sport and, more recently, in church reorganisation. We still search for identity and connection – witness the growing interest in local history and heritage. That is why when we hold our area gatherings in Sixmilebridge, the first step is to write up the history of that area. People are extraordinarily proud to acknowledge the achievements of the generations that preceded them. There are everyday indications that people want to come together as a community. Often, sadly, it is highlighted when tragedy strikes, as in the small fishing village of Union Hall in Cork when the *Tit Bonhomme* boat went down. The community simply took over in coping with the loss and the search for the fishermen. My friend John Quinn was so impressed by the reaction of the Clarinbridge community to the tragic death of photographer Joe Lane at a car rally that he wrote:

Love in the Midst of Sadness

Someone had to direct the traffic
With quiet efficiency.

Someone had to mow the field
To help us park with ease.

Someone had to clear the yard
And erect a large marquee.
Someone had to greet the crowds
For this broken family.

Someone had to make the sandwiches
Brew the coffee and the tea.
Someone had to bake the buns and cakes
And serve them constantly.

And someone will no doubt say
'Aren't ye great to help them through!'
And someone else will answer
''Twas the least that we could do'.

In all the dark and all the pain
How beautiful to see
Such witness of real love
Of true community.

John Quinn

Tragedy apart, there is now, I think, an undefined movement that people want to take control of their own lives. For many, the world has moved on too quickly. The twentieth century brought us into the world of institutions. We experienced the growth of centralised power, nowhere more visible than in government. We began to believe it would do everything for us and we moved away from doing things for ourselves. Across the country, semi-state bodies and other powerful institutions represented major change in the way we used our resources and the way we were expected to live. The Church and the banks were equally powerful institutions.

It is a different world now. We are all aware of the scandals, the breaches of trust, the waste, that have plagued modern Ireland in recent times. Those were betrayals of today's young generation by those who abused power and the trust placed in them. That generation is now calling attention to civic morality and to the concept of people taking control of their own lives. Music, song, dance and the arts generally give them the opportunity to do that. As I write, the Leaving Cert examination is about to get underway. We need to move away from rote learning, the points race, the 'jug-and-mug' approach to schooling. It is imagination and creativity that will save us, not facts. No primary or secondary school should have formal classes without serious consideration of that school's immediate world – the community, the local resources, who creates jobs, who works there. Our own village, Sixmilebridge, reminds me of a beehive. There is so much going on here. We underline the importance of our young people connecting deeply with this.

In trying to get out of our current difficulties, we seem to be relying on the same principles and measures, the same style of leadership which created the difficulties originally. In a paper to the 2010 Céifin conference entitled 'The Culture Change – a Living Systems Perspective,' Paula Downey made a very telling observation:

> What we are witnessing is not a recession, but the early stages of a systems failure, the collapse of a culture that is based on a dysfunctional story. We are a culture in confusion because we are the first generation to have reached the limits of what economic and material growth can provide to a developed country … While those who lead our institutions have taken us to the brink, our deeper problem is not the nature and quality of those in leadership positions, but the 'story' they believe and use to guide their decisions.

In Paula Downey's view, the 'storytellers' must keep us focused on our most primitive needs, creating false wants to convince us to keep on consuming. The result is we have become a debt-ridden society, because the systems that shape us have taken away our sense of responsibility and have disconnected us from who and what really matters, who and what gives meaning to life – our inner selves, family and community.

I fully support this analysis. All through the Celtic Tiger years we were encouraged to get into debt and consume, because that is what kept the wheels of the economy turning. We have now come to the end of that story. It is a far cry from a past when we were all reared to save. You could only spend when you had saved. That was the key to our work in the Rural Resource Organisation in the 1970s – cultivating the habit of saving. Now in this era of austerity we are told to go back to saving once again.

So maybe the past has a future – 'the past' meaning pre-major institutions. We need to be careful however, not to heap our own sins on the sins of our fathers. There is a certain rejoicing now in debunking politicians, bankers and clergy, but the real danger lies in deluding ourselves into believing that we are more honest, more trustworthy or more enlightened than those we condemn. We will only know that if and when we are given responsibility. If we can have a new kind of leadership that will have a facilitating nature and give us responsibility, then we must be prepared to take that responsibility. We cannot wash our hands and say this mess is not our problem. It is our problem, hence the importance of community in facing it. But we do not start from where we are now. We cannot build a civilisation without roots. If we fail to think more deeply about where we are going and if we fail to identify some of the things from generations past that have relevance today (see 'Remembering Mary Ryan'), we risk building a society that is not based on reality but on abstractions, with a life that is lived without root or depth.

We live in historic times. The reconstruction of society that is required will have to take place from the ground up. You don't attempt to build a house from the roof down. We won't build a future from Brussels nor from the global world but we will build it community by community into a movement, a way of life in which people will live by their own hands and skills, rather than by being totally dependent on people elsewhere. Health services will continue to be crippled if we continue to overdepend on them, instead of taking a little from Mary Ryan's world and looking after our own health and nutrition. Equally, in 'spiritual services', we have a lot of ritual in organised religion but we need to connect more deeply into the contemplative, meditative world.

> As the body cannot live without food, so the soul cannot live without meaning. Victor Frankl described this so well when he pointed out that some level of meaning was the only thing that kept people from total despair and suicide during the Holocaust. Humans are creators of meaning, and finding deep meaning in our experiences is not just another name for spirituality but also the very shape of human happiness. (Richard Rohr, *Falling Upward: A spirituality for the two halves of life,* John Wiley & Sons)

In 1992, Jacques Delors, the eight President of the European Commission, stated that a successful Europe could not be built on economic know-how alone. If Europe did not have a soul, a spirituality, within ten years, he claimed, the European project will have failed. Twenty years on it still doesn't have that soul. The project would seem to be failing. Spirituality implies a desire to be connected with something beyond the self. For some, the word is interchangeable with ethics, values and trust. From here on, we will need to be a generation that can be trusted, that will have values like truth and honesty to guide us. Likewise for the organisations that order our lives. There is a lot of evidence that the hunger for spiritual values is not being met by organised religion. This represents a huge challenge for the renewal of the Church. The recent Eucharistic Congress was hopefully the beginning of realising that challenge.

Every culture maintains the existence of a soul – that lifegiving presence that we find hard to define. The Celtic Tiger drained that energy from us. It convinced many of us that we did not need one another, nor did we need God. We only needed money and so we became an economy totally dependent on debt. A recent survey by the Irish League of Credit Unions stated that 1.8 million households are barely surviving. We desperately need hope for the future. The *soul* we need now is tied into community and into drawing energy from our past. That has nothing at all to do with going back to 'poor but happy' authoritarian times. The twentieth century brought us colonialism and clericalism. The way forward for the twenty-first century is surely community.

TWENTY-TWO

Cahercalla – A Community Hospital

One of the purposes of this book is to underline the importance of the local and of initiatives undertaken at local level which respond to the real needs of people. One such initiative in Co. Clare has been Cahercalla Community Hospital.

In 1951 the Sisters of St John of God opened Cahercalla House as a nursing home. It was subsequently upgraded to hospital status, providing maternity services, and for thirty-eight years the sisters, together with nursing and ancillary staff, touched the lives of the people of Clare and adjoining counties through their devoted work and service. Cahercalla has always been known for its friendliness and homeliness, allied to the high standard of nursing and the personal attention to each patient. The sisters brought a very special spirit to the hospital and the staff brought a huge commitment to the physical, psychological and spiritual well-being of the patients. I had personal witness of this when my own mother spent her last months in Cahercalla before she died there in 1980. Our family will be forever grateful for the loving care she got from the entire staff, including notably Fr McLaughlin, the resident chaplain. Long before the hospice movement, Cahercalla was pioneering special care for the terminally ill. Many Clare people also saw the first light of day there, until the maternity unit closed in 1979.

Through the 1980s, falling numbers of vocations put the sisters' resources under stress and by 1989 they felt they could no longer run the hospital. Initially, the Mid-Western Health Board expressed an interest in using Cahercalla to provide services for the mentally ill. The hospital staff were not happy with this and organised a public meeting on Cahercalla's future in September 1989. A large crowd attended the meeting, which was chaired by solicitor Brian McMahon. Bishop Michael Harty asked me to represent him. It was quite a heated meeting and when it became obvious that no conclusion would be reached on the night, I asked the superior for an opportunity for a small group to reflect on the hospital's future. She agreed and the meeting selected Brian McMahon, Dr Frank Counihan and myself to look at the options. Discussions with the Health Board were suspended pending an alternative for the hospital's future. The group held a number of meetings and were later joined by Dr Frank Hassett and the notion of a community hospital emerged. Frank Hassett had particular experience of such a venture which recognised that the medical needs of people in a defined area (e.g. Co. Clare) should, where possible, be met within that area. Our research indicated that Cahercalla could provide nursing home, minor surgical, rehabilitation, screening, consultancy and hospice services on a community basis.

The sisters postponed negotiations with the Health Board to discuss the concept of a community hospital with us. This would be a major undertaking for the group, the sisters and the community. As a group, we had no money and as yet no clear mandate, so in January 1990 we held a public meeting in the Queens Hotel, Ennis. It was agreed at that meeting that the people of Co. Clare would purchase Cahercalla. From there progress was slow until in November 1991 a contract was signed and a deposit of £20,000 was paid. Major fundraising was now required and in 1992 we invited the then Minister for Health, Mary O'Rourke, to launch the Cahercalla Community Hospital Appeal. We were heavily dependent on the trust of the people of Clare and of the sisters, who agreed to stay on until at least 1996. We were also engaging with banks and potential financial contributors. A purchase price of £650,000 was agreed and this, combined with the development of new facilities, pushed our target to one million pounds. A special fundraising committee was set up. The property title was vested in trustees representative of different areas of the county but excluding any vested interests. The property would now be a charitable trust. A Board of Management was established and this facilitated the phased withdrawal of the sisters. I was asked to take on the role of Chairman of the Board. Though I was reticent to take on another role, I agreed to do so. I had been advocating all my life for local involvement in meeting the needs of people and talking about the untapped potential of local community. The community-hospital approach put these ideas to work and I wanted to support it in whatever way I could.

Adopting the community hospital was also congruent with the ethos of the Sisters of St John of God. It ensured that their concerns for staff and long-term patients would be honoured. There would be no suggestion of the hospital being used exclusively for profit. A succession of meetings worked on the viability of the hospital and the continuation of arrangements with the Voluntary Health Insurance Board.

I have gone into some detail on the story of Cahercalla in order to underline the size of the undertaking. A few people, whose opinions I would value, later told me that we were mad to have taken on the project. It may have seemed so to them, but we as a board never saw it that way. I always believed that in addition to the public and private sectors, there was a third sector – the voluntary – which could prove crucial to meeting the needs of a community. Through the years, under many different guises – development associations, Tidy Towns, co-operatives, citizenship groups – the voluntary sector has been involved at local level. Unfortunately, it is not encouraged by political or statutory bodies and when the public and private sectors grew strong, the voluntary sector tended to be undermined and a dependency on the public and private sectors was promoted, often extending to European and global levels.

When Cahercalla was finally established as a community hospital in 1995, its services were limited to an eighty-bed nursing home. Since then it has developed into a unique entity, adding on-day surgical and outpatient services and hospice care. The day-surgery and outpatient service is now staffed by nineteen highly-qualified consultants with a team of nurses, providing a wide range of procedures in oral surgery, general surgery, urology and gastroenterology. These services ensure that the community has much of its healthcare needs met at a local level, thus obviating the need for lengthy travel or waiting lists.

In 1997 the conversion of the old convent extended the nursing home beds and initiated a hospice service. The board invited 'Friends of Cahercalla' to help assess the community's needs and how the hospital might respond to those needs. This led to a further state-of-the-art twenty-bed extension, which included en-suite rooms, social space and a family room offering overnight accommodation for relatives. This development highlighted the inadequacy of the older parts of Cahercalla under modern nursing home standards. A capital programme of four million euro was drafted to address this problem and finance was acquired at a difficult time for business generally. This project was completed in 2013.

Fundraising is obviously an important part of the Cahercalla initiative, especially with regard to the hospice. This service is available to all, irrespective of means. At all times the board has fostered strong links with the community, encouraging volunteer input in the delivery of services and in fundraising activity. Cahercalla is their hospital, providing services for them. They are aware that they have a stake in this community initiative. It is now a large employer, with over one hundred and twenty people working in the hospital and it provides business for many local suppliers and service providers.

The emphasis on the local is the key to this initiative. Hospital and hospice care are provided in a spirit of service, offering total respect for the person and his/her needs. There is an atmosphere of homeliness and friendship and the location is close to family, neighbours, local doctors and clergy. Surgical services and consultancies are provided without having to join long queues. All of this is vital when the provision of centres of excellence and the centralisation of services are receiving a great deal of attention at government level.

'om left: Harry, his father Michael, his brother Seamus and his sister Anna.

Harry's mother and father, Bridget and Michael Bohan.

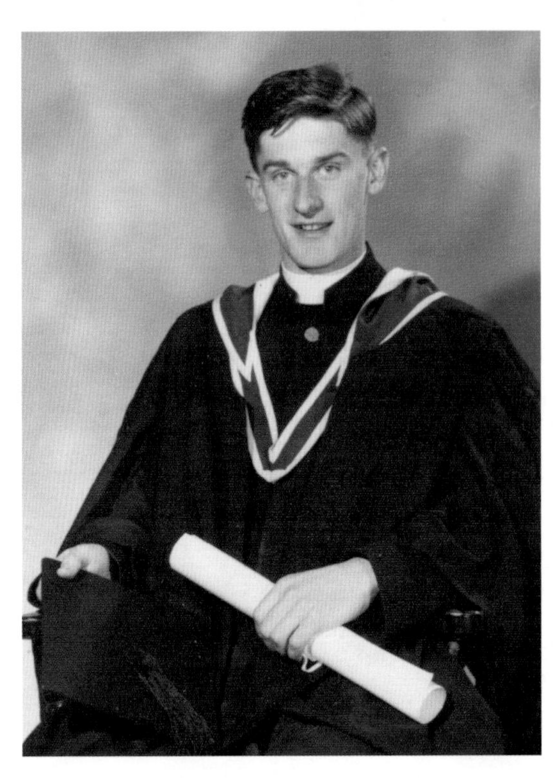

Harry on graduation day

Harry's ordination day. From left: brother Michael, sister-in-law Tess, father Michael, Harry, mother Bridget, sister Anna and brother Seamus.

Opening of the first Rural Resource housing scheme, in Feakle. From left: Harry, Brendan Travers, Joe Moloney, Taoiseach Liam Cosgrave and Bishop Michael Harty.

each Liam Cosgrave turning the sod at a Rural Resource housing scheme.

Opening of the Sixmilebridge Mart, 27 August 2011.

Opening new wing at Cahercalla Community Hospital & Hospice.

Harry at one of the Céifin conferences – 'Is the future my responsibility?'

Harry with John Waters, Paul Tansey, Maurice Neligan and Bishop Donal Murray.

Harry at Clare–Kilkenny hurling match.

Harry with the Clare hurling manager, Davy Fitzgerald.

Left: 'Area gathering' at Kilmurry.

Right: Harry with Jimmy Corry.

The scene at one of our 'area gatherings'.

Left: Harry's Jubilee, with Bishop Kieran O'Reilly and Bishop Willie Walsh.

Right: Harry with Teresa Houlihan at the Jubilee gathering.

Back row from left: niece Aisling, sister-in-law Tess, niece Aideen, brother-i
Tim, nieces Áine, Helen and Ciara.
Front row from left: sister Anna, Harry, brother Seamus and sister-in-law B

TWENTY-THREE

The Gaelic Athletic Association

The Gaelic Athletic Association (GAA) is an extraordinary organisation. Founded in 1884, it has straddled three centuries. When it was founded, the people of post-Famine Ireland were poverty-stricken, spiritless and seemingly without a future. Yet in that remarkable period in the latter half of the nineteenth-century, with the coming of the GAA, the Gaelic League, the Land League, Catholic revivalism and the Co-operative movement, the people found a new spirit, a reason to live and to hope. Today, as we experience a period of recession, there is a lot we can learn from the contribution those movements made to the country's revival. Balancing the local with the global is one of our great challenges today.

All through its existence, the GAA has been bound up with a sense of place and belonging. It has bonded people together and given them stability. Today, we live under a cloud of instability and confusion. We have witnessed a loss of trust in institutions, spiralling unemployment, the continuing collapse of a culture shaped by consumerism and borrowing, the undermining of family and community and the erosion of values which connect us to our inner selves, to one another, to Creation and Creator. If we are to bring stability to society and security to our own lives, we will need to rediscover a sense of place and take pride in who we are and the culture that shapes us. Without a vision, people die.

The value which the GAA has placed on the native place is unequalled. It is imperative now that the GAA rediscovers its own ethos and spirit, both for its own sake and because of the influence it can have at a time of instability and insecurity. For the emigrant in London or New York, Boston or Brisbane, it is very often the local team and parish which still bestow identity. The GAA needs to prioritise the club over the county team – the current trend would seem to be in the opposite direction – as the club, the parish team has been the foundation on which the organisation is built.

The wonder of this Association, for well over a century, has been the manner in which small communities and people of humble backgrounds have become household names throughout the country and beyond. Small rural parishes – Ballyhale, Kilmurry-Ibrickane, Loughgiel, Clarinbridge – have taken on the dimension of greatness through their achievements on the GAA playing fields. Small can not only be beautiful but successful, proud and independent too. It is unlikely if our country has ever needed such examples of greatness, self-reliance and leadership more than it does now and in the coming years. It is equally unlikely that any organisation other than the GAA could more effectively drive home the message that a nation can only be built community by community, from the ground up and never from the top down.

Just as humble places have been exalted through the GAA, so too have humble people. We think of hurling heroes – Christy Ring, Mick Mackey, John Doyle, Jimmy Smyth and numerous others from the past. These men were great, not just because of their achievements on the pitch, but also because they remained men of their own people who never lost sight of their origins and roots. It gives me great heart to see that hurling heroes of today hold the same values.

One of the hallmarks of the GAA has been its ability to counter discrimination at any level. At a time when the gap between rich and poor continues to widen in our society, it is worth remembering that this amateur sporting organisation has always brought people together from town and country, from rich background and poor. It has served as a unifying force, classless and all-embracing, and in so doing has played an important role in community building.

Another hallmark is the GAA's ability to make Irish people comfortable with themselves and their traditions. Before the advent of television, the Association provided an arena for all the people in a community to focus on. On a wider level, it has played an important part in restoring a national self-confidence, providing ordinary people with an opportunity to organise themselves and articulate their ideals. It has been aptly described as 'the Parliament of the People'. Civil War and party politics took a back seat in the GAA. Muintir Na Tíre was probably the only other movement which involved all sections of the community to a similar extent. So, after decades of being told how unfit for self-government Ireland was, the GAA encouraged an independence of spirit among the population, a pride in their distinct culture and in the economic and political potential of Ireland itself. It has, through events like Scór, fostered talents in music, drama, dance, folklore and traditions, and has given people of all ages the opportunity to participate on a very wide scale in all those aspects of our culture.

Probably the greatest strength of the GAA has been its amateur status and the ideal of voluntarism. There is an ongoing debate about the possibility of payment to managers, coaches and maybe players, but voluntary effort has been the cornerstone of the GAA and to abandon it now would be an incalculable loss. The club remains the central and most important unit of the GAA. It is vital that this is redefined practically within the Association and is not allowed to be undermined by any other unit. The GAA is not just about Croke Park, Thurles or Clones. It is fundamentally about every small community that proudly organises and runs a club successfully.

A major concern now is the pressure on county players. Recently, John Mullane, one of the greatest forwards the game has ever seen, retired from inter-county hurling at the age of thirty-two. He spoke frankly to the media when he indicated that the demands placed on inter-county and club players are extreme. He went so far as to say that the mental strain was enormous as well as the physical. The conclusion which people are coming to is that the fun is going out of the game, that more and more players are being forced to retire at a younger age and that the dual player (one who plays both hurling and football) is fast becoming a thing of the past.

Unfortunately, there seems to be very little appreciation at administrative level for the fact that burnout has to be the result of all this pressure. Another serious consequence is the fact that the club will continue to suffer and could eventually be damaged beyond recovery. If that happens, then the GAA will have lost its significance as a movement which was founded on the basis that the local is all-important – the place where people live and can have a sense of pride and belonging. The GAA is primarily a movement which connects to the local for its lifeblood.

The family and the school are vital to the life of the GAA. Clubs need to introduce parents to the ethos and spirit of the Association, not just in offering coaching to children but in promoting neighbourliness, togetherness and a real sense of community. With regard to schools, there has been a tendency for some schools to be in communities and not of them. Again, the GAA has a lot to offer schools, not only in the practical aspects of their games, but also in connecting them to place and heritage.

As a society, we stand at a crossroads. There is much confusion about which direction we should take and which values we should promote. The concepts of community and neighbourliness are being eroded. For a century and a quarter, the GAA has thrived in building and cementing communities, building local pride and establishing a sense of place. If, as I believe, we are to balance the local with the global, through rediscovering community and working together in a co-operative spirit, then the ethos and example of the Gaelic Athletic Association is there for us all to emulate.

TWENTY-FOUR

Hurling and Me

In my childhood days my next-door neighbour, the late Paddy Loughnane, was a great hurler. He won five county championships with Feakle and he was a regular on the county team. From the time I was four or five years old, Paddy and his wife Nellie would bring me, and maybe one or two others, to hurling matches in the 'back-to-back' trap. Nellie had a special box for me to sit on. Paddy used to tell me that I was one of the youngest to be brought to matches in those days.

The GAA, and hurling in particular, was very much part of my growing up and indeed my life. I played hurling from a very young age as did most young lads of my time. We knew no other game. It has also been very much part of the life of this country – community by community. The thrill of the game, the pride in the local place and the sense of togetherness were all ingrained in me from a very young age.

All through my college days, I would envy Tipperary their hurling success whenever I drove through that county. A fellow student from Tipperary once told me he felt superior to us. 'Why?' I naively asked. 'Because we win All-Irelands and ye don't.' While inter-county success for Clare was non-existent, with the exceptions of an All-Ireland in 1914 and a National League title in 1946, there was considerable interest in club hurling, and particularly strong rivalries between clubs e.g. Clarecastle and Newmarket; Feakle and Scariff.

I returned from England in the early 1970s. In 1973, the county hurling team was being managed by the late and great Matt Nugent. The pride in the local place and sense of togetherness had been ingrained in me and having returned to my roots, I was young and brash enough to get a few people to support Matt. We were never officially appointed to do anything we just drifted into the 'background team'.

In 1974, I took over as 'manager' without any selectors – although the term 'manager' was not in vogue then. We had the same love for the game in Clare as in any other county. But it was evident that we would have to bring organisation and structure to that game, develop skills and encourage the right attitude to training and preparation and instill belief and togetherness in players. I had no illusions. I knew it would take time, hard work and self-belief but the signs were good early on. I was ambitious for the team and I wanted them to be ambitious too. In that year, we beat Tipperary in the Munster semi-final but lost to Limerick in the Munster final. Whilst acknowledging we were beaten, getting to a Munster final was a significant achievement. In the first ninety years of the GAA, Clare had appeared in only five

Munster finals. Over the next decade, they would appear in five more finals.

It became clear to me that a certain type of player was needed to play at county level. Not everyone, not even a very good hurler, is cut out to be a county hurler. A certain amount of character is demanded. I set out to comb the county for such players and moved away from the traditionally strong clubs. I added fellows here and there to our panel from junior clubs – Jackie O'Gorman from Cratloe, Pat and Enda O'Connor from Tubber, Colm Honan and the late Tom Crowe from Clonlara. If someone told me there was a brilliant wing-forward playing for his club, I would go to watch him and imagine him playing on Colm Doran from Wexford in Thurles or further afield in Croke Park. He would need that almost indefinable quality – a good head as well as a good heart.

In 1976, we reached the National League final against Kilkenny which ended in a draw but we were badly beaten in the replay. While the replay was disappointing, the first game had given us the confidence to believe we could compete with the 'big boys' and that we could take this progress forward. The two years that followed were great ones for us. In 1977 and 1978, we won the National League, beating old rivals Kilkenny on both occasions. A League title may not be the pinnacle of success but winning two of them 'back-to-back' was huge for us, as it had been so long since Clare had won anything.

After the 1977 League final, I had invited Justin

McCarthy from Cork to join the backroom team as a coach. Justin made a great contribution to skills development. He was very meticulous in his approach, right down to the choice and care of hurleys, often mending them himself. We also had Colm Flynn as physical trainer so we were well prepared for the Munster Championship.

We disposed of Limerick and Tipperary before facing Cork in the Munster final before a crowd of 44,586 people (memorable also for the fact that the 'gate takings' were stolen in a robbery during the second-half and never recovered). After conceding a penalty, which Cork scored, in the opening minute, we regrouped and looked like we had what it took to win the match but just before half-time, disaster struck – our full-back, Jim Power, was sent off. With that, our chance was gone and Cork went on to win the game by five points. I felt the team was *right* that year and that if we had won in Munster, we had the players and potential to go on to take an All-Ireland.

It was our misfortune, however, to come up against, what many people rate as, the greatest ever Cork team which included such players as Jimmy Barry-Murphy, Charlie McCarthy, Tim and Johnny Crowley, Ray Cummins, Tom Cashman, Seánie O'Leary, Gerald McCarthy and many more. On top of that, they had the legendary Christy Ring as selector! After the final whistle blew, he shook my hand and said: 'Stay with them. You are young and you are doing a good job.' 'I don't know a lot about it,' I replied. 'I don't know much about it myself,' the great man said with a chuckle. I often quoted his remarks afterwards to people who thought they knew everything about hurling!

After another League title in 1978, we faced Cork once more in the Munster final before a massive crowd of 54,181 people, the biggest attendance since 1961. Once again, with neither side playing particularly well, we came up short by two points. Cork went on to win their third All-Ireland in a row, a truly great team. If only they had emerged at a different time!

In 1979, we lost the League semi-final and I decided to step down. I was now heavily involved, pastorally, retreat-giving, and in the development of the Rural Resource Organisation (RRO).

For all that, I was enticed back to manage the Clare hurlers again in 1980. We were back in a Munster final in 1981, only to fall to Limerick, specifically to Joe McKenna's three goals. I still think we could have won that match.

I stepped down a second time and Seamus Durack, who had been goalkeeper in my time, took over a few years later. He asked me to join him as a selector which I reluctantly agreed to do. In 1986, we narrowly lost another Munster final to Cork, our fifth in a decade. Defeat sets you back, but I never stopped believing that we had the potential to win something. Perhaps seeds were sown for the great days of the nineties.

Managing a county team is not an easy task but I

enjoyed it. I devoted an enormous amount of time to it, together with the RRO, so the chat was often either hurling or housing. During my term, I tried at all times to bring organisation, togetherness, belief, pride and commitment to the panel. In turn, it brought home to me the absolute passion that exists for the game.

The rivalry between clubs could be intense especially between near neighbours, Clarecastle and Newmarket. I remember fellows togged out in opposite corners of the dressing room. Initially my biggest task then was to get the players thinking bigger than club loyalties. From the beginning too I felt it was important to be there for the players in different aspects of their lives. Some people would say I was too close to the players but it was important to me to be interested in them not just as players but as people. I always felt that players, who gave so much to the GAA, didn't get enough respect at decision-making levels in the organisation.

Liam Griffin, former Wexford hurling manager, used to quote me as saying: 'If there never was a player, the GAA would still meet.' In other words, there are two GAAs – the players and the administrators. Players come and go but (some) administrators can seemingly go on forever. There is much talk today of 'player power'. Thinking back, we had an early example of 'player power' in Clare. In 1976, some members of the County Board felt that we were not making enough progress and there was a move to replace me. The players had gone on a trip to the USA and whilst there, they met. They wanted me to continue as manager and on their return made their views known. The backing of the players meant everything to me. I would not have stayed on without their support.

Winning All-Ireland titles in the nineties, is something that will never be forgotten by Clare people everywhere. We had our heroes – Anthony Daly, an inspirational captain, Davy Fitzgerald, the Lohans, Seánie McMahon, Jamesie O'Connor and Ollie Baker – to name but a few. Clare had finally arrived and old men and women could now die happy. This in turn encouraged underage hurling. The County Board introduced development squads. It is now wonderful to see under-8s, under-10s and under-12s participating in hurling blitzes here in the parish of Sixmilebridge. We have come a long way.

For all that progress, I have a number of concerns about the game. An obvious one is that it is confined to too few counties, certainly at the 'top table'. The GAA is a massive organisation, mainly because of its ethos. In the drive for training and skills development, that ethos should never be ignored – the sense of identity, of belonging, of Irishness. The organisation's connection with club and community is vital. I worry also about over-coaching. I worry when I see players look to the sideline for instructions rather than being given the freedom to express themselves as best they can. Brian Cody does the latter with Kilkenny. I admire Kilkenny hurling – they come, they play the game well and they go home. There is no fuss. They are well-grounded.

Because sport is such a vital part of life, players need to be careful not to be drawn into the celebrity world. Hurling is for everyone at all levels. It is about *we* more than *I*. It is about more than medals and cups. Winning is, of course, wonderful, but the most important thing is playing the game well. The modern game is parsed and analysed by the media. So many people are influenced by the analysts' views now but to use the old cliché, hurling is a simple game.

Looking back on hurling in my life, as a player and a mentor, the memories are wonderful. I do not like singling out players but in my management days with Clare, I was lucky that we had such outstanding young players like Sean Stack, Ger Loughnane, Sean Hehir, Johnny Callinan, Enda and Pat O'Connor and Colm Honan with the older warriors like Jim Power, Jackie O'Gorman, Noel Casey, Seamus Durack and Mick Moroney. I think too of Jimmy McNamara, a brilliant half-forward who captained one of our League-winning teams, who rarely gets a mention nowadays and Johnny McMahon who came on the team, almost by accident, as a wing-forward and won an All-Star award as a corner-back. I could go on …

In 2003, Anthony Daly was appointed manager of the Clare senior hurling team and he invited me to join his backroom team as a selector. I enjoyed a new lease of life. Anthony was an outstanding manager and was unlucky not to have achieved success, going so close to defeating Cork in the 2005 All-Ireland semi-final and Kilkenny in the 2006 All-Ireland semi-final. Men like Brian Lohan, Seanie McMahon, Colin Lynch, Jamesie O'Connor and, of course, Davy got a new lease of life when he took over.

In terms of my time as a selector with 'Dalo' ... I think I could write another book about that! The man himself is larger than life. He is never short of a word and he could sing for Ireland. He is an extraordinary leader of people – his captaincy of the Clare team in the 1990s was hugely significant in the winning of the two All-Irelands. He was and is a Clarecastle man through and through. He loves the place, the people and above all its characters. I used to say to him 'Dalo, ye are not a parish at all. Ye're a tribe.'

It was a massive experience to work with him. I wasn't a young fella when he asked me to come onboard. I thought he was mad and there is a bit of that in him. In fairness that makes him the man he is. I, like many others, have huge time for him as a hurler, a leader and a human being. My experience of working with him was for sure 'an experience'.

TWENTY-FIVE

Being Ill

On 2 June 2011, I underwent a colonoscopy. When a tumour was discovered and the dreaded word 'cancer' was mentioned, my immediate response was 'I'm not surprised.' In the preceding months I had to deal with a high number of deaths from cancer in the parish. Between calling to the dying, presiding over funerals, and visiting grieving families, cancer was in the air and in my head. It was happening to so many, so why not me?

I was sent to the Galway Clinic under the care of two excellent doctors – Professors McAnena and Keane. The tumour was removed in its entirety and I would not need chemotherapy. My relief was tempered by the fact that I had to face further surgery for an aortic aneurism. Again I was fortunate to be in the care of a terrific nurse, Orla O'Donnell, at whose wedding I had officiated. She was so practical, so positive and so efficient. Her care for me underlined the special contribution nurses make to the health service. They are dealing with the rawness of life and their greatest quality is compassion, which is not easy when working under stressful conditions with a range of very sick people. We are in their debt.

In November I was back in hospital, this time the Limerick Regional. This was, again, in relation to my aortic aneurism which was being regularly monitored. By now it required major surgery. It was a difficult operation and I was warned to take plenty of rest afterwards. I was never too good at taking rest and foolishly resumed my ministry before Christmas. Willie Walsh helped out but the damage was done. On 28 December I officiated at the wedding of the niece of a contemporary of mine. Fr Hugh O'Dowd had died suddenly the previous August and left a gap in all our lives, so I was happy to be there for his niece, Ann. In chatting to people after the ceremony, I suddenly felt the power draining from my left leg. On New Year's Eve I was back in Limerick Regional Hospital for more surgery to correct a stent that was blocking the blood supply to my leg. My surgeons, Paul Burke and Eamon Kavanagh, were fantastic and proved themselves to be good and caring men. Home again and after a short period of rest, I resumed parish duties.

Towards the end of July while celebrating my birthday with a family lunch, I felt a numbness and a weakness in my right leg. I struggled through a month's mind Mass that evening. The next day I went to Bunratty Folk Park to meet two Canadians who had asked to have their marriage vows renewed. I waited an hour. They never turned up. My condition was worsening all the time. I had to return to hospital, this time the Hermitage Medical Clinic in Dublin. Dr Clarke came to see me and was so concerned that he asked the surgeon, Mr Mundhovan, to examine my case. Another scan revealed that the stent was not functioning, having been blocked again. I was transferred to St James's Hospital where Mr Mundhovan and his team performed a lengthy and difficult procedure on me to restore the blood flow.

I am writing this sixteen days later and I am still in hospital. I am not sure what the future holds but I do know that long periods of physiotherapy, careful monitoring of blood levels and plenty of rest are vital. To have confidence in those who care for you plays a major part in healing. I cannot speak highly enough of the staff at St James's. Mr Mundhovan is quite simply a genius – decisive, confident, humble, thoroughly professional. His team are brilliant. When I praised them, a young female doctor simply replied, 'They care' – and it is so true. The nurses and staff, led by ward sister Iris Curtin, oozed enthusiasm and confidence. The happy co-operative system on the floor made all of us patients feel good.

Having been in hospital five times in the last eighteen months, I can say the same about the staff in the Limerick and Galway hospitals. It was easy to have confidence in them. We are very fortunate to have so many concerned and caring people working in the health service. Obviously, the structure of the service needs overhauling because the system isn't working. We hear praise of other systems like that in France, but ours doesn't seem to work. I don't know why but maybe, as with other systems and institutions, the culture which has allowed so many over-bureaucratic and hierarchical authorities to evolve needs to be reviewed and adapted to the needs of our time. The dedicated personnel are still there. We need to ensure that many of them are not allowed to drift away in frustration and disillusionment.

We as citizens are also duty-bound not to overburden the health services. Better lifestyles, more exercise, careful diet – all would ease the pressure on the health system. Then there is the terrible abuse of Accident and Emergency centres by people under the influence of alcohol and drugs. It is not only an abuse of doctors and nurses' time but a serious abuse of their own persons.

These are just some reflections, written in a hospital room, based on my own experience over a very difficult year. The devoted care of medical staff, the support of parishioners, the prayers and messages of so many people, have all brought home to me the great potential, kindness and essential goodness of people. We should never underestimate or forget that.

TWENTY-SIX

In Search of Wisdom

Saturday, 18 August 2012. I am sitting in my room in St James's Hospital. Not feeling the best this morning. Coping with post-operative feelings, weaker limbs, pain is not easy. Must stay positive. There's a lot of time for thinking in hospital. Outside of my own problems, I am reflecting on a crisis-torn world – crisis in the economy, in the Church, in institutions, in personal lives. Where will the solutions come from? We need wisdom. We desperately need wisdom. Where is the source of that wisdom? I have just been reading from the Book of Wisdom in my breviary:

> For I am a man who is weak and short-lived, with little understanding of judgement and laws; even if one is perfect among the sons of men, yet without the wisdom that comes from you, he will be regarded as nothing … (Wis 9:5–6)

It set me thinking. In this information age, more and more *wise* people claim to know it all. Who were the wise people I knew?

Just then a nurse, Helen McElhinney, came in to take my temperature. We got talking. She told me she had two uncles who were priests, both now deceased. One was Henry Nash, late of Mullinahone, Co. Tipperary. I couldn't believe my ears. Here was part of the answer to my question. If I was to single out a truly wise man in my life, Henry Nash would be that man. I have quoted one of his sayings so often – 'It isn't easy to say a few words at a man's funeral, if you've never stood in his kitchen.'

In one simple sentence, Henry underlined what was fundamentally important to the priest's ministry. Pastoral theologians have written books and lectured students about it but here it was expressed in the simple words of a humble man. Learn to listen, listen, listen – and hear. It's easy to jump in with the solution without hearing the problem. Listeners are scarce, while the opinionated and judgemental are plentiful. The wise nurse or doctor must listen to your story before writing your prescription.

Later in the Morning Prayer I read:

> May what is false within us
> Before your truth give way
> That we may live untroubled
> With quiet hearts this day.

Pretending to be who we are not, putting on a show, image over reality – this is what is false within us. To thine own self be true. In the midst of illness, wisdom continues to reveal herself to me.

Tuesday, 4 September 2012. Home again. Good to be here, but the road to recovery is long and slow. Still thinking of Henry Nash and wisdom. Where can we find more of that? The Church is in crisis and has opted to go through a period of retrenchment. It is an easy option, in my opinion. How much do clerics know about the real world? Are our leaders capable of reading the signs of the times? Do they have prophetic instincts or are they just keeping the organisation ticking over? There is every indication that people are walking away from that Church. It may seem a terrible thing to say but that Church could be in the throes of death …

Over a hundred years ago, Cardinal Cullen introduced a chapel-centred, clerically-dominated Church. It was strong for a century but has been on the wane for the last forty years. If we don't accept that and move to a different kind of Church, we are doing serious injustice to the real Church of Jesus Christ. So if the clerical Church must die, there will be rebirth. Something has to die, and be let die, for something else to grow. That rebirth into a new sense of faith can only happen if we stop over-relying on a chapel-centred Church. Don't get me wrong – the church is a sacred space at the heart of the community but we must also look elsewhere. What about the faith that was home-centred, connected to nature and the seasons? I think of the wisdom of farmers and seamen who could *read* the sun, the moon, the seas and the mountains. That faith, connected to nature and the hand of God and nourished by Celtic spirituality, is vital for our future.

Sadly, there is little evidence that our leaders are cognisant of this. Today in the post I got the September issue of *The Furrow*. There is an excellent article on bishops by Fr Brendan Hoban. He is looking for people with 'creativity, imagination, an ability to approach reality at an oblique angle, a prophetic disposition, an independent mind, an ability to connect with the rhythms of our times. These crucial constituents of leadership don't seem to be valued requirements for episcopal office at present'.

I totally concur with that list of requirements for leadership. They are needed not only by Church bishops, but in our politicians, in our banks, in society generally. Sport has shown us examples. In leading their teams to an All-Ireland final, managers Jim McGuinness (Donegal), James Horan (Mayo), Jim Gavin (Dublin), Jimmy Barry-Murphy (Cork), and Davy Fitzgerald (Clare) have met those requirements. But as for the Church, Brendan Hoban says the opposite is the case. The people who are in favour of leadership now, he claims, are those who are 'in favour of traditional confession, against the ordination of women, support *Humanae Vitae*, lively Marian devotion, and never write or say anything that might be interpreted as critical'.

I respect Brendan Hoban. He is not a crank. He loves the Church. Rather than attempt to silence him, we should listen to his wisdom. It is blatantly obvious that a clerical power that held sway for over a hundred years is now dwindling away. Let it off. Let it go. Let new buds emerge. They are emerging in many parishes and people are responding. Let them not be buried.

The movement towards a rebirth will have to cope with a breakdown of confidence in all forms of authority and touch back to old values which are based on a wisdom which emerged from years of experience and observation. We need to rediscover the faith that our ancestors had – deeply connected to place, home, story and the presence of God. A faith that connects to the real people in their lived experiences. This will lead to a new way of being Church. We could call it a Christian community. It will be a slow process, finding its way in the dark. It will be slow but it will come, because the happenings at local level will touch the hearts and minds of the people. Happenings like our 'area gatherings', despite the fact that we are never asked about them … What do they mean? Are they making sense?

I couldn't sleep last night (again) so in the small hours I began reading an account of the late John O'Donohue's Easter Dawn Mass at Corcomroe Abbey in the Burren. John asked all present to be silent in the darkness so that they might dwell on the areas where they needed Easter healing and hope. He blessed the four elements – earth, air, fire, water – before moving into the ruined abbey for the Consecration of the Mass. I thought it was such a powerful connection – linking the profound mystery of the Resurrection to the emerging dawn and the beauty of the Burren. At the same time John was connecting with the modern world – with the healing that each one present needed. Where is John now when we need him to help us identify the riches that emerged from our Celtic past? I lay back in my bed and tried to enter that world, seeking healing for my own wounds.

A friend of mine who is engaged in technology told me recently that his biggest worry is that technology continues to advance without an ethical foundation. The Ireland of the Celtic Tiger era was oblivious to ethics. Individualism and quick profit were its dominant values. A Sunday newspaper recently featured twenty-four people who made huge money in the Celtic Tiger days on the back of debt. They built fanciful houses and created property empires. What were they at? It is time to debunk individualism. In a post-modern world maybe we can only move forward on pre-modern values. That is why I keep remembering Mary Ryan. We are social animals. We belong to communities, to a society. *Ar scáth a chéile a mhaireann na daoine* – 'people live in each other's shadows'. That is what society and the Church of the future must build on.

I must reiterate that this is *not* about 'the good old poor-but-happy days', *not* about nostalgia for a former time. Never! It is about recovering a value system, an ethics, a morality that seems to have disappeared in modern Ireland and that has been replaced with the type of raging individualism and greed that brought the country to its knees. It is about finding new ways of living and working that draw from our past.

As for the Church, for me the future is local and adapting to that and facilitating it is vital. Paul VI said we cannot have religion without inculturation. It must permeate the culture. John Paul II in his millennium document (*Novo Millennio Ineunte*) said the Church must connect with local culture. Reaching out, rather than circling the wagons, seems to me to be the way forward. Henry Nash standing in a man's kitchen. John O'Donohue's Easter Mass in the Burren. Our area gathering in Sixmilebridge Mart. That is the Church. That is the Faith. The people's Church. The people's Faith.

Postscript

Brendan Hoban's article on bishops and leadership suggests a bleak future for the Church without new vision and thinking. How encouraging then are the recent words of Pope Francis when he spoke to a gathering of papal nuncios in Rome about the criteria they were to apply in proposing new bishops for appointment:

> Be careful that the candidates are pastors close to the people, fathers and brothers, that they are gentle, patient and merciful; animated by inner poverty, the freedom of the Lord and also by outward simplicity and austerity of life, that they do not have the psychology

> of 'Princes'. Be careful that they are not ambitious, that they do not seek the episcopate … but above all that they are able to 'watch over' the flock, to keep watch, imbue hope, that they have sun and light in their hearts, to lovingly and patiently support the plans which God brings about in His people.

I am not naive enough to think that these words of Pope Francis will make an overnight difference but they are grounds for hope that appointments will be made with a pastoral Church which is close to the people.

TWENTY-SEVEN

Jesus – The Person

Still in search of Wisdom

In the world of politics today, concepts such as fiscal rectitude, openness, transparency, accountability, governance and leadership seep into every discussion. They are all valid concepts for a way forward out of our present difficulties, but it is obvious that much more is needed. The values and the culture of our political, religious, administrative and financial systems require radical change.

Two thousand years ago, religious, political and administrative systems had also failed. The world was in trouble and needed the intervention of God. He sent His own Son to bring a totally different value system into that troubled world. Those values became what we know as Christian values today. Jesus said simply that He was the Way, the Truth and the Life. To rediscover those values and what they mean for us today in practical terms, we need to turn to the person of Jesus. We have been overly concerned with the practice of our faith to the neglect of who or what we believe in and why.

For many years now I have met up with a group of my Maynooth classmates on a regular basis. We socialise, have a meal and have genuine faith-based discussions. Recently, we gave serious thought to the question Jesus Himself posed – 'Who do you say that I am?' We turned to a book entitled *Faith Maps* by Michael Paul Gallagher, in which he takes ten major religious thinkers and asks how each would point us in the direction of the Christian faith. In his introduction, Gallagher writes:

> Faith involves the whole story of God, as revealed in Jesus Christ. I recall a remark by an Irish journalist to the effect that in pubs you can sometimes hear arguments about God or the Church, but hardly ever about Jesus Christ. Pub discourse on religion tends to stay on the surface. But what I want to explore here takes us into logic and onto another wavelength.

That 'other wavelength' was what our group was trying to reach. Each of us took a different chapter of the book to analyse and present to the group. One of the group chose the chapter on Bernard Lonergan, a Canadian Jesuit philosopher and theologian who is also qualified in science, economics, mathematics and classics. As a group we were excited by what we heard about this important thinker:

> Lonergan saw that theology was hopelessly out of touch, with its emphasis on topics in which most people

> had no interest. A whole new world had come into being, leading to a crisis of culture, rather than a crisis of faith. Instead of starting from Scripture or Church statements, theology should begin with the experience of being transformed by God's love … There has to be a radical transformation that is fundamental to religious living. Real religion is conversion.

What a pity we had not touched into this kind of theology years ago! Here was an explanation of why the Irish Church found it difficult to have an influence on the shaping of the new Ireland. The new world of industrialisation, technology (especially communications technology) and free education led to a crisis of culture for us. The surveys tell us we are still a nation of believers but, in the case of Catholics, the faith of the majority is seriously undernourished, which in turn is a reason for the irrelevance of the Church. We need, as Christians, to get back to beginnings and rediscover Jesus. We talk a lot of moving to a new model of Church, a Christ-centred Church. But is that enough? It seems that this journey must begin with rediscovering Jesus – who He was, who He is for us, at a personal level. This means that we must live out a process of permanent conversation at that level.

'Who do you say that I am?' Jesus asked His disciples. In the midst of our current crisis, this should be our question too – who is Jesus for me now? In evolving a new model of Church, as we busy ourselves with the important concepts of participation, collaboration, governance – perhaps we should begin with the concept of conversion to the person of Jesus. Once we commit ourselves to coming back to His person, to understanding His message, to grasping His deepest insights, to feeling His love for God and people and to staying with Him as part of the process, then all the other steps towards renewal fall into place.

When we remind ourselves that God loves the world so much, then we see the face of God in Jesus and we see the world with all its pain and struggle in a new light. When I look back over my own life now, I realise it was the person of Jesus, the One who walked this earth, who kept me in a relationship with God. It is the world He loves, not religion, not Churches as such, but people. He did not set up an institution but a movement, a community. 'I come to do the will of My Father … I am the Way, the Truth and the Life …' So we must ask ourselves what is the will of God for us now. In turning to Him who is the Way, the Truth and the Life, we find the vision.

In practical terms, Jesus gave special emphasis to compassion, performing acts of kindness to relieve suffering and pain. He paid special attention to the abuse of power, to people who said one thing and did another. He also emphasised the power of prayer, of moving away from the busyness of life to spend time in reflective communion with His Father. Following Jesus means coming near to people in the real, concrete situations, casting off our indifference, speaking a language people understand and identifying their needs and responding to them.

It is important that we see Jesus as present, really close to us. Our image of Him will shape the way we hear what He is saying to us in the gospels, how we preach His word or hear it preached, how we celebrate the sacraments and nourish our faith, how we understand *real presence*. When we talk of a new model of Church maybe the first step to renewal is in that process of conversion to Jesus – who He was, what He stood for, the example He gave – and having Him as the beginning, middle and end of the Church. Let us leave ourselves open to the Spirit, putting our trust in Him and allowing Him to prayerfully shape our future …

In my own life I have been fortunate to have had the seeds sown by my parents and to have been inspired by people who have brought me close to the One Prophet – Jesus – who is the centre of our existence. They pointed the way for me, creating an awareness in me of a God who has to be understood as signifying compassion, not power, a God who cared for people in their need, a God who spent time in prayer. He was Jesus.

TWENTY-EIGHT

A Man Apart

Cardinal Carlo Maria Martini SJ, biblical scholar and former Archbishop of Milan, died on 31 August 2012. For me he was one of the great open-minded thinkers of the post-Vatican II Church and an influential voice that commanded attention. I was a great admirer of his and would have loved to have met him.

In his last interview, just days before his death, he said:

> The Church is tired in affluent Europe and in America. Our culture has grown old. Our Churches are big. Our religious houses are empty. The bureaucracy of our Church is growing out of proportion. Our liturgies and our vestments are pompous ... The Church is two hundred years behind the times. How come it doesn't rouse itself? Are we afraid? Fearful instead of courageous ...?
>
> I am old and sick and I depend upon the help of others. The good people around me make me feel loved. This love is stronger than the feelings of disillusionment that every now and then I feel towards the Church in Europe. Only love can overcome tiredness. God is love.

Every word of that is meaningful for me. As I write I am struggling to recover from major surgery and I too feel I can only cope with the help of good people who surround and support me and make me feel their love. As for the Church, Martini's questions are so relevant. Who has the courage now to give leadership and direction? Martini was obviously not anti-clerical. He loved the Church but it was the Church of Jesus Christ and His people. He was head of a huge diocese of five million people and he did all in his power to reach them. He spoke to them each week on the diocese's own radio station. He connected people to the Christian message and to Christian values. For him the Church had to have a practical and real presence in the modern world. He bore witness to this in his own life, combining an extraordinary scholarly life (he spoke eleven languages) with a deeply-practical core to his pastoral life.

Christ had to be at the centre of the people's world and Martini achieved this in many ways. One of the most special ways was to set up a contemplative meeting with Jesus by listening to His Word, reflecting on its richness and connecting it to the daily lives of people. Every Sunday afternoon thousands flocked to the Cathedral and churches of Milan to partake of this great nourishment of the soul – among them a high proportion of young people. Little wonder that when Martini's body lay in state in the Duomo in Milan, over 200,000 people came to pay their respects.

In the early 1990s Milan and indeed all of Italy was

rocked by a deep political crisis. There was large-scale corruption in business and politics. While most of his fellow bishops stayed quiet, aligning themselves with the corrupt Christian Democracy party, Martini spoke out courageously against the corruption. In 1992 he was chosen as Milanese Man of the Year. The citation for the award was interesting …

> In the past year in which Milan was rocked by a deep crisis that seemed to have made the city lose confidence in its own identity, Cardinal Martini, with the primacy of the Word, with the missionary impulse, with the exercise of charity, with an incisive and constant participation in the civil and political affairs of this city, with a strong teaching given from his chair of Ambrose and Charles (Borromeo), has infused courage and hope, but he has also recalled each person to responsibility and to personal and social duties in the spirit of Christian love …

Here we have a description of a Christ-centred Church. 'God loved the world so much that He sent His Son …' The Son would bear witness to the truth, show the way and connect people with one another. Carlo Martini was following in the path of the Son.

From the first days of his episcopate, he wrote and spoke to his people on a wide range of social and religious issues, from business ethics to women's rights. His definition of Church made a difference in the real world. He read the signs of the times and responded.

Had we enjoyed his leadership in Ireland, imagine what he would have had to say about the banking and financial worlds here. Imagine the kind of local Church he would have been promoting. Imagine how he might have addressed a Church that is, by and large, out of touch with modern Ireland. Is he not a clear example of how we need to examine seriously what we mean by *renewal* – not as a further extension of clericalism, but as the real participation of lay people? People who are at the heart of business, political and community life, who bring the concepts of Christian ethics to the real world. Who knows the real world better than the people who inhabit it? Who understands family life better than parents? As Brendan Hoban said recently on radio:

> The future is the parish. Priests are limited in their gifts. All around them are gifted people. Release those gifts! Release that energy!

While I am critical of an over-clericalised Church, I want to acknowledge that some of the finest people I have known in my life were and are clerics. Many of them in post-Vatican II years promoted a people-centred Church, open to the inspiration of the Holy Spirit – men like Fr Seamus Ryan, one of the great priests of our time – a man of courage, humility and deep faith. These were men who loved the Church and were critical only of a Church that would not allow an honest search for change and renewal – change that is embedded in the way Christian communities exercise their Christianity.

In his book, *What is the Point of Being a Christian?* Timothy Radcliffe underlines this position:

> All the Christian Churches have in recent years been making a big push to spread the Gospel. Certainly in the Catholic Church there has been a lot of talk about evangelisation. Dioceses and parishes have drawn up ambitious plans to let people know about our faith. Usually these have had little effect. We talk about love, freedom, happiness and so on, but unless our Churches are seen really to be places in which people are free and courageous, then why should anyone believe in us? Jesus spoke with authority, not like the Scribes and Pharisees, and His authority was surely His manifest freedom and joy. His words made an impression because they were embedded in a life that was striking, reaching out to strangers, feasting with prostitutes, afraid of nobody ... We will waste our time in producing more documents, videos, radio and TV programmes, unless we work to make the Church a place of evident courage, joy and hope.

If faith is to make a difference to people's lives, it will mean giving those people responsibility for the Christian community they are part of. It will mean that clerics must let go of control and give themselves the freedom to be and to do what is required of them in a changed Ireland. We live in very difficult times. The scandal of abuse rumbles on. Church leaders have little credibility. But out of crisis comes opportunity. Give the people back their Church and they will respond with careful facilitation and participation in initiatives that make sense to them. We have much to learn from a leader like Carlo Martini – a man apart. We have 'men apart' here at home too, bishops and priests who can be real leaders, honest and courageous enough to move towards the Church that Christ founded and away from the 'bad old days' of clericalism.

TWENTY-NINE

BENEDICT AND FRANCIS

I was finalising the contents for this book when our Church and indeed our world experienced two extraordinary events. The first of these happened at the beginning of February 2013 when Pope Benedict XVI decided to step down to allow a new man to take over. Benedict's papacy was dominated by spiritual discipline yet troubled by a certain amount of controversy. He spoke, as Pope, for the last time on Wednesday, 26 February. His last speech was remarkable.

Obviously deep thoughts went into his parting words. He left critical messages for all of us as to where the Church is now and where it needs to go. He said he felt like Peter and the Apostles on the Sea of Galilee. He felt the Lord was asleep. At times he felt alone in an over-centralised Church. Even his closest aides were not with him. (Pope Benedict's butler was arrested in 2012 for stealing his private letters.) He clearly referred to a Church that needed reforming, starting with the Vatican itself.

Benedict will be remembered for many great things – not least of which was the three wonderful books he wrote on the life of Jesus (the *Jesus of Nazareth* series) – who He was, the power of His life and message, and His centrality to the life of the Church and our understanding of it. He was obviously saddened that Christian values were not connecting in a more meaningful way to life, especially in Europe and the Western world. His belief in Jesus is very deep and he passionately believes in nourishing that belief through prayer.

In deciding to step down, he has left the Church with an extraordinary legacy. In his parting words, he didn't shirk addressing difficult questions about the Church. He indicated that the Church has to face up to the challenges from within and without. His legacy of humility, compassion and single-mindedness will hopefully serve the Church of the future well.

The second event was the appointment of a pope from South America. On 13 March 2013, Cardinal Jorge Mario Bergoglio of Buenos Aires, Argentina became the 256th Pope, taking the name Francis. Neither his appointment nor the name he chose were expected.

Cardinal Bergoglio wasn't mentioned in the first ten likely candidates. Straight away, he left his mark. He has been described already, as exactly the kind of man for our times – a symbol of hope in times of crisis in the world and in the Church. He reminded us that the Church has lost contact with people. To reconnect he picked up from Benedict in that he pointed out that the Church is about Jesus – *His* Presence, *His* values, *His* way of connecting. He immediately identified himself with the poor and marginalised. He got rid of some of the trappings of power: He had Mass on Holy Thursday in a prison for young offenders, he brought three thousand homeless people to the Vatican to pray with him. The world seemed surprised. These ways of connecting come naturally to him because they were Christ's Way.

> I was hungry, I was naked, I was in prison, I was homeless and a stranger and you fed, clothed, visited and housed me.

The fact that the media and the world were surprised was an indication of how far we had gone from the central message of Christ.

In a very short time, Pope Francis represented new beginnings, new hopes. In words and actions he has stressed that the Church he leads is about Jesus Christ and not the pope. It is about service, not being served. He is already showing the way, but it is agreed that his leadership and his witness will be effective only when we on the ground, community by community, follow the same route. That will involve us in a lot of pain, suffering and sacrifice because Christ's Way is the Way of the Cross and it is only then that the rest follows.

THIRTY

Bishops who made a Difference

Earlier I mentioned Brendan Hoban's critique of the episcopal appointments today. I have to say I have been extremely fortunate in the men who were bishops of Killaloe during my time in the priesthood. I have already mentioned the foresight of Bishop Joseph Rodgers who recognised the changes – economic, social and religious taking place in the 1960s. Bishop Rodgers died suddenly in 1967 and was replaced in the same year by Michael Harty who was Senior Dean in Maynooth. A native of Toomevara in North Tipperary he had an intimate knowledge of life at local level. He recalled me to the diocese in 1968. He not only, as I have already recorded here, facilitated me to get involved in exploring initiatives relevant to the emerging face of our region but he himself supported it step by step and encouraged it both publically and privately. He clearly recognised the concept of 'development' as an integral part of the work of the Church.

Bishop Harty had a particular interest in the concept of small community development, with villages and towns central to this. He encouraged it. He was aware of the vital importance of having a balanced population, with younger faces in Church, schools holding on to their numbers and teachers, and the GAA, of which he had a particular interest, benefiting enormously. He was also interested in co-operatives which processed produce from the land. He kept in contact with the leaders of these co-ops and with rural organisations in general. If he had occasion to go to meetings in Dublin he would often use the occasion to have lunch with key personnel from the world of agriculture.

He showed a particular interest in two industries. A factory in Scariff, Co. Clare, producing chipboard, using the raw material from timber harvested in surrounding farms and employing up to one hundred and fifty people, was experiencing problems. Local people were concerned. They contacted me asking if I could meet the Minister for Forestry and ask Bishop Harty to get involved and come with me. When I rang the Bishop's house I was told he was with the dentist in Shannon. I rang the dentist. He told me the Bishop was on the chair. I spoke to him. He agreed to come to Dublin straight away. We met the minister and later met one of the big 'players' on the Board of the factory. Both these meetings led to a rescue plan for the factory.

My second memory was to do with the possibility of a major milk powder plant being established in Co. Clare. This involved several meetings of all the dairying interests in Clare and beyond. Bishop Harty not only attended all these meetings but also made available a site for the project outside Ennis. Eventually the project didn't get off the ground but the initiative led to the transfer of milk in Clare from the Dairy Disposal Board to Golden Vale Co-operative.

These are but a few examples indicating not only the serious interest which Bishop Harty had in the life of people on the ground, their growth and development, but also the respect lay people had for him. They recognised not only the concern he brought, his genuine support but also his knowledge and expertise. In other words, in all of this he knew what he was talking about. There are many other examples of his interest and involvement in development. He had a particular interest in Shannon Airport. In fact one of his last public statements, which he and I prepared together was about the airport.

He was a great Church leader. There was widespread respect for his wise, calm decision-making. He was highly-regarded among his own episcopal colleagues. He had an acute understanding of the relevance of the Vatican Council documents. His interest in good Liturgy was enormous. Practically every Church building in the diocese was renovated during his time and a few new churches were built. He believed good Liturgy in a bright building was crucial not only in developing the spiritual life of people but also community morale.

These are just a few of the qualities and contributions Michael Harty brought to our diocese. He had a particular interest in schools and teachers – again vital in contributing to local communities, to the future careers of young people. He also encouraged priests and lay people to take courses in social services, Church music, etc.

Above all, at a personal level he was extraordinary. He was kind, gentle and caring but also appreciative of efforts made. When he died we knew we had lost somebody we deeply appreciated as our leader, and one who left his mark in the life of many people.

Willie Walsh had been appointed coadjutor bishop meaning he would have the right of succession. Sadly, Michael Harty died before Willie was consecrated. At his ordination as bishop, Willie asked me to preach the homily. I was chuffed but nervous. As he got up to say the few words himself his little skullcap fell off. He picked it up and said 'this could be a sign of things to come'. And it was. He didn't pay too much attention to the trappings of the office, i.e. titles or dress. He took the words *'Cinealtas Chriost'*, meaning the 'Kindness of Christ' as his motto. He lived it.

I suppose I could say – it would be hard to find another Willie Walsh. We are overjoyed with the appointment of Francis as Pope. His simplicity, humility and love of the poor have captured the hearts and minds of people everywhere. Willie Walsh has all of that and more. Willie cared – full of heart – honest to the core. He is certainly a role model for what a Christian leader should be.

His love of and care for the poor and the marginalised

was best exemplified in that the travelling community became his closest neighbours. There were times when ten to twelve caravans would have occupied the lawn in the front of his house, many of them taking up a permanent place on the grounds. And he became a genuine neighbour to them but not only to them, to others too who were less well off.

Bishop Walsh was very much loved by the people of Killaloe. What you saw was what you got. He was always available to people. Their concerns became his. He put them, their cares and their worries at the very heart of his ministry. He did this because he first put Christ at the heart of it. I would say he often asked himself in different situations 'what would Jesus Do?' As a pastor he was superb. He would have concentrated, for the most part, on the pastoral and the spiritual, devolving a certain amount of administration, finance issues to others – enough to give him space to concentrate on what he regarded as priorities.

He was an extraordinarily brave man in that he was always prepared to say or do what he believed was right without looking over his shoulder at higher powers. Willie's propensity to say what needed to be said (what others were often afraid to say) frequently landed him in trouble. He believed in speaking honestly. His integrity demanded that he speak openly about issues such as child sexual abuse, the role of women and the situation of separated and divorced people in our Church, and the Church's attitude to gay people. No doubt he paid a heavy price for his openness as it sometimes brought him into conflict with Rome. We were especially fortunate to have had him as our bishop at a time when the abuse crisis was at its height. He was comfortable enough to speak credibly about this issue when most of the bishops were in flight from it. His honesty won him the affection of priests and people who greatly admired his integrity.

When Willie was appointed he continued to support initiatives in which I was involved. He supported the Céifin movement, the search and debate it was involved in and he attended every conference. Indeed, one of the outstanding inputs to the conferences was made by him in 2002. He often told me he felt he hadn't the same understanding of development issues as Michael Harty, but he continued to trust and to support.

I came to work closer with him when he asked me to take up the role of Director of Pastoral Planning. He played a huge part in putting the plan together. He had a real sense of the primacy of baptism, that our shared baptism made all of us equal participants in the Church, with a shared dignity as members of Christ's body, but also with a shared responsibility for the future of the Church. He was very clear that structures were not ends in themselves but only mechanisms for communicating the message. The structures could never get away from the Spirit, the core of the message of Christ.

The implementation was the next step. For whatever reason, it was difficult. Maybe we weren't skilled enough in bringing priests and people with us. Maybe it was a major step forward which we didn't fully appreciate. I felt that the priests were central to implementing the plan. Willie often told me that he wasn't one for pushing the priests. It wasn't in his nature. We did our best and we made some progress.

Willie Walsh is now retired but busy. Since this retirement I feel I've gotten to know him not as a bishop but as a friend. I deeply appreciate his kindness to me during my illness and his willingness to fill in for me in the parish at that time.

Kieran O'Reilly is now our Bishop. He is a Corkman. He came from afar. He was Superior of the S.M.A.'s , based in Rome. His appointment was a big surprise to us. It came out of the blue. It must have been a difficult appointment for him, coming to a diocese like Killaloe with its own history and culture about which he knew nothing. It must also have been difficult to succeed a bishop as popular as Willie Walsh. But he came to us bringing his own gifts and understanding of Church as a missionary, a perspective that in time may have much to say to a changing Church reality.

Kieran has settled well – he is a personable man. He seems determined to do things his way and to put his stamp on planning for the future. He is a good administrator and is gradually putting structures and people in places which effectively mean devolving responsibilities to other people.

He is a believer in encouraging people to do things for themselves. He gives priests and people, at local level, their head to solve their own problems and do things for themselves. In this he is encouraging priests and people to take responsibility. A pastoral plan under his direction has been launched for the diocese in September 2013. It is based on a listening programme carried out over a year. It places a special emphasis on the need to nurture Christian community. It points out that our diocese has fifty-eight parishes but in reality there are one hundred and fifty-six Christian communities in which the Eucharist is celebrated every weekend. The plan is asking us to address the future of these communities. How will they survive in the emerging reality where we will have far less priests in ministry than we have now? Only by encouraging these communities to take responsibility themselves will they survive. The same theme comes up again – local communities taking initiative, taking responsibility, being the Church in their own place.

Conclusion

We have been fortunate in our diocese with the bishops we have had in my lifetime. To be able to say that is important. But there were others outside of the Church who gave leadership which I admired and to whom I am deeply indebted, people whose thinking and vision I believe went way beyond the norm.

In fairly recent years people like Tom Collins stand out, Tom Barrington before that and Ivor Browne. Diarmaid Ó Donnabháin and Jim Lyons were exceptional in the field of education at local level, as was Michael McGrath in agriculture. Women like Paula Downey, who spoke twice at Céifin conferences, and Emily O'Reilly, new European Ombudsman, speak passionately and powerfully about Irish society and offer profound critiques of the systems in which we live.

THIRTY-ONE

Returning to the Source

Joe Martin, a great friend of mine, and his wife Marie were down with me lately. Joe and I were in Maynooth together. We went in to Maynooth on a September day in 1956. Joe was from Tyrone and I from Clare – two very different cultures. We became great friends. We had common interests, not least of which was the GAA. Joe wasn't ordained. He left a few months before ordination and went on to become head of one of the Education Boards in Northern Ireland. He met and married Marie, who is a serious contributor to the use of technology in the world of education.

They came down to celebrate my Golden Jubilee with me and a cross section of people in the parish on 21 June 2013. That day we were chatting about this book. They asked me if I had a title and I mentioned a number of titles we were considering. We talked about it and a few days later Joe rang me to suggest: *Swimming Upstream*. It sounded good. We reflected a bit on the main theme running through the book. Joe then asked me – 'do you know much about salmon – the fish'. I said 'not a lot but I do know salmon comes in from the ocean, the wide expanse of water to swim upstream. In doing this they return to the source, come back home to spawn'. That is good, I thought. Nature shows us how things happen – the natural way. I began to think how important it is to recognise that and to learn from it. The importance of the local, the source. Home in the face of the global.

So, in a way this book is about reflecting on the source for the most important things in life. I began to think further. Back in 1993 I wrote a book, titled *Hope Begins at Home*. It tried to reclaim the importance of *source* for human life itself, the shaping of that life, the centrality and potential of the human being in the development process and the living out of life. In the face of technology and the power and influence of big organisations, the empowerment of people seemed vital. I tried to point to a future based on years of practical experience. I claimed that a sense of powerlessness was underlying our national malaise, with people's families and communities no longer having the responsibility for shaping their own lives. People were looking then for a new vision, a return to roots, to truth and spirituality. Many have now become very cynical of people in high places. They are looking for hope now more than ever and so search for that which will give meaning to life.

In that little book I tried to search for a way forward under chapter headings which traced the history of the family, and how it changed through the decades – the family as the school of Human, Social, Christian living; the role of schools; the importance of helping ourselves, the idea of giving power to the people and hope in a changing Ireland.

Twenty years on from the time I wrote that book I am now more convinced than ever that there is an urgent need to challenge the conventional wisdom as articulated by dominant forces in our society. Most people agree that economic, social and pastoral planning can't take place without listening to people. Institutions which shape society need to be changed if society is to be transformed. The leadership of the future will have to be a facilitating leadership rather than a dictatorial or overly authoritative one.

At the outset I indicated that my only purpose in writing this book is that it might generate some thoughts and debate on the potential of 'ordinary' people. Having spent my life working with people – centred work – I am reminded of Mick Cooley's dictum that he has never met an 'ordinary' person, only 'extraordinary' ones. I can say, with absolute conviction and humility, that I have spent my life working with extraordinary people. They are people who are at the heart of getting things done in their local communities. However, these people are on no central stage in Irish society. In fact, their opinions are rarely asked or considered. They are farmers, unemployed men and women, professionals, industrial and office workers, and retired people amongst others. Many belong to families and to community groups, to associations and to organisations. More are people who want to do their own thing: They are people, many of them, who could achieve high levels of personal creativity.

Year after year annual reports of agencies, big companies keep on coming out with the well-worn clichés about people being the greatest resource of a firm, a bank, a government body, even a Church. Yet, these same organisations – public and private – put more time and money into planning the next office block or piece of equipment than developing the vast skills and creative talents of what they keep saying is their greatest resource.

A number of years ago I heard Bishop Michael Harty, who had invested a lot of time and money renovating Church buildings, say we must now focus on the development of people. It was a beginning but didn't get very far. As power and decision-making got more and more centralised in the hands of a few it was important to keep people in the dark. Power-seekers know that without knowledge and competence, it is difficult to have confidence to challenge. It is important to them to communicate in a language people do not understand. The Church did it for years. We are expected to understand but how can people understand without meaning?

I am writing this on a Sunday at the end of June 2013. The running media story of the past week has been the shocking disclosures from the Anglo Tapes which effectively uncovered the culture of a bank. This was a culture which treated people with disdain, a culture which has long forgotten that banks are only strong because they control the money of ordinary people and now they cynically demand that taxpayers should bail them out. It's a culture which applies not only to banks but to all organisations and institutions which have lost touch with people. The time has come now not for *reformation* but for *transformation*. This certainly demands a return to obvious solutions beginning with attitudes and systems which respect people, take account of their experiences, listen to their views and include them in decision-making.

To endorse the urgency of this it is worth quoting our president, Michael D. Higgins, in the aftermath of the Anglo revelations. He said he had often referred to the terrible damage inflicted on Irish society by the aggressive individualism and self-interest of a speculative economy:

> This week voices from the past have been heard which serve to highlight behaviours and attitudes at the very root of that failed economic model. They do not make for easy listening. But let us be certain of one thing: these are not the voices of the people of Ireland. The attitudes they reveal are not shaped by the people of Ireland. The behaviours they reflect are not characteristic of the people of Ireland.

The Anglo revelations attracted a lot of attention abroad. The president said the people of Ireland were shocked and dismayed that a culture of greed and recklessness emerged in some of our institutions, a culture which was not in keeping with our core values as a nation.

The Irish people, who are rightly recognised for their fortitude, work ethic and courage, will take us out of this present crisis. The authentic voice, spirit and values of Ireland will be restored.

The clear message is: Give this country back to its people – give the Church back to the people of God. The question now is are we ready to take responsibility?

People must first experience freedom to come to a relationship with God – their God – without a Church understanding of what is 'right theology' etc. In this independence can people trust in the simplicity of Christ – His humility, His honesty. Harry touched on this but didn't quite get there.

Words that have Sustained Me

There is nothing new under the sun …
(Ecclesiastes)

Your vision will become clear
only when you look into your heart;
who looks outside, dreams;
who looks inside, awakes.
(Carl Jung)

Who will rear the next generation?
(participant at a Céifin conference)

Today many things indicate that we are going through a transitional period, and it seems that something is on the way out and something else is painfully being born. It is as if something were crumbling, decaying and exhausting itself, while something else, still indistinct, were arising from the rubble …
(former Czech President, Václav Havel)

They didn't talk God. They did God.

(Emma Spence at the funeral service of her father and brothers)

The Church is bound to no particular form of human culture, not to any political, economic or social systems. Hence the Church, by her very universality, can be a very close bond between diverse human communities and nations, provided these trust her and truly acknowledge her right to true freedom in fulfilling her mission.

(Pope Paul VI, Gaudium et Spes, *'The Church in the Modern World')*

The opportunity of a lifetime has to be taken in the lifetime of that opportunity.

(Anonymous)

We are a culture in confusion because we are the first generation to have reached the limits of what economic and material growth can provide to a developed country ... While those who lead our institutions have taken us to the brink, our deeper problem is not the nature and quality of those in leadership positions, but the 'story' they believe and use to guide their decisions.

(Paula Downey)

It isn't easy to say a few words at a man's funeral,
if you've never stood in his kitchen.
(Fr Henry Nash)

Gross National Product does not allow for the health of our children, the quality of their education or the joy of their play. It does not include the beauty of our poetry or the strength of our marriages; the intelligence of our public debate or the integrity of our officials. It measures neither our wit nor our courage; neither our wisdom nor our learning; neither our compassion nor our devotion to our country; it measures everything, in short, except that which makes life worthwhile.
(Robert F. Kennedy)

You give but little when you give of your possessions.
It is when you give of yourself that you truly give.
(Kahlil Gibran)

It is simply unthinkable that our final destination could be the cul-de-sac of complacent consumerism when we are the first generation to have within our reach the great destination of an egalitarian republic in which the strong are driven by a restless and unselfish duty of care

for the weak and where every life is given the chance to fully blossom.
(Mary McAleese, Céifin 2005)

Happy the home wherein lies three generations.
(Japanese proverb)

Isn't it odd that our economic growth depends on producing more and more things that we don't need, so that we can pay more and more people to do the work to produce these useless things? It seems odd to me that we cannot make money and wealth out of good things like better health, better education and better environment.
(Charles Handy, Céifin 2001)

In measurable ways societies don't work as well where we are not connected to one another.
(Robert Putnam, Céifin 2002)

Be careful what you wish for.
It might come true!
(Anonymous)

The day is not far off when the economic problem will take the back seat where it belongs and the arena of the heart and the head will be occupied or preoccupied by our real problems – the problems of life and of human relations, of creation and behaviour and religion.

(John Maynard Keynes)

We must be the change we wish to see in the world.

(Mahatma Gandhi)

I know from my experience in Ireland that the thing I admired most was the authenticity, the genuineness of the people and the fact that relationships matter more than things.

(Stephen Covey, Céifin 1999)

Don't stop doing things 'cos you're getting old, 'cos you only get old when you stop doing things.

(Thora Hird, actress, at the age of ninety)

If we command our wealth, we shall be rich and free; if our wealth commands us, we are poor indeed.

(Edmund Burke)

It's the few who make things happen, the many who watch things happen and the majority who don't know what's happening.
(Anonymous)

Kant put it differently. People, he said, have *dignity*. Everything else can be exchanged and hence has *value*. People cannot be exchanged.
(Robert E. Lane, Céifin 2001)

A sense of place means a sense of society.
(Joe Lee)

It is wrong for a greater organisation to hold to itself the right of making a decision which a lesser one is already qualified to do for itself. Subsidiarity necessitates a relationship of trust, not control.
(Pope Pius XI, Quadragesimo Anno, *'The Principle of Subsidiarity')*

Put out into the deep … The programme is the same as ever. It is the plan found in the Gospels and in the living tradition – (but) it must be translated into pastoral initiatives adapted to the circumstances of each community

– it is in the local churches that specific details of the pastoral plan can be identified.

(Pope John Paul II, Novo Millennio Ineunte, *'At the Beginning of the New Millennium')*

'Tis a gift to be simple, 'tis a gift to be free.
'Tis a gift to come down to where we ought to be.

(Hymn: Simple Gifts*)*

There is a time for everything
And a season for every activity under the heavens;
A time to be born and a time to die,
A time to plant and a time to uproot,
A time to kill and a time to heal,
A time to tear down and a time to build,
A time to weep and a time to laugh,
A time to mourn and a time to dance,
A time to scatter stones and a time to gather them,
A time to embrace and a time to refrain from embracing,
A time to search and a time to give up,
A time to keep and a time to throw away,
A time to tear and a time to mend,
A time to be silent and a time to speak,
A time to love and a time to hate,
A time for war and a time for peace.

(Ecclesiastes)

Refuse to identify with negative, blaming, antagonistic, or fearful thoughts (you can't stop having them).
(Richard Rohr, Immortal Diamond*, John Wiley and Sons)*

Always seek to change yourself before trying to change others.
(Anonymous)

History is not made by cynics. It is made by realists who are not afraid to dream.
(Anonymous)

A dead thing goes with the stream. Only a living thing can go against it.
(G. K. Chesterton)

The salmon goes upstream to generate new life.
(Anonymous)

The Changing Role of the Priest

Address to the Knock National Novena, August 2011

> It was the best of times, it was the worst of times, it was the age of wisdom, it was the age of foolishness … it was the spring of hope, it was the winter of despair, we had everything before us, we had nothing before us.

So begins Charles Dickens's novel *A Tale of Two Cities*. In it he referred to England at a time of industrial revolution and also France in revolution. His words could easily be attributed to these days. These are days of immense change. New needs have to be met and new questions have to be asked. We became smart scientifically but without wisdom and humility. The concept of priesthood has changed dramatically. This has come about because of the scandals in the Church and because of the fewer and older priests in the job. Tensions exist within the priesthood – between those who cling to a clerical form of priesthood and those who see the Church as a community with the priest as a facilitator or animator.

The tensions which many priests are experiencing have their roots in history. At the end of the Middle Ages the priesthood was in crisis. It was unable to respond to the challenges of a new world. The response to this crisis led to an extraordinary renewal in the priesthood. A new spirituality, new seminaries, a more relevant and profound theological formation emerged. That was the Council of Trent. But that understanding of priesthood has been showing signs of crisis for some time. The Second Vatican Council of the 1960s tried to address this. One of its more powerful documents – *Gaudium et Spes*, 'The Church in the Modern World' – emphasised the importance of reading the signs of the times and connecting with the reality of life for people. Interestingly, a new Ireland also emerged during that decade.

It is probably true to say that the Irish Church never engaged enthusiastically with the core messages of Vatican II, confining itself mainly to liturgical changes and ignoring the call to engage with a new Ireland, thus withdrawing from the real world. There were exceptions to this and Monsignor James Horan was one of them. The Church in Ireland, however, ignored the uncontrolled growth of cities, the massive housing estates, the high-rise flats, the emergence of big organisations such as banks and government bodies – all under the guise of progress. As our view of progress came to be one of climbing the ladders of knowledge and power, based on greed and uncontrolled competition, the Church in Ireland was silent.

There has been an obvious ethical vacuum in Ireland for some time now. Values such as truth, trust and honesty were sidelined in the face of the power of the marketplace. But the most serious crisis of all for the priesthood and the Church now is how to rid itself of clericalism and authoritarianism, of which the sexual abuse scandal is but a symptom which gripped it. How is our Church to become a humble, listening Church, which connects with the needs of the people and facilitates their participation, professionally and voluntarily? How is its credibility to be restored and the trust of the people to be regained?

If we look back to the beginning of Christianity, we see that Jesus was a man of His time, a man of the people, a man who shared deeply in the life of the people and responded to their needs both spiritually and practically. The Church that Jesus founded was a community first of all, not a hierarchy. Vatican II supported this idea with its central thesis that the Church is the people of God. If we agree that the Church is the people of God, then the implications are enormous, especially for the role of the priest. Top-down leadership cannot be a part of this model. Top-down has failed miserably. It has failed in the banks and it has failed in big organisations. It is about the culture of control. It is obvious that we need a new culture of authority from the top to the local parish.

Jesus established a community of loving equality to make His word and His ministry present in the world.

How does the priest become a facilitator of this vision? He must be able to read the signs of the times and to connect to the mystery of Christ, His word, His presence, His witness, with the reality of life within that community. The priest must, in the words of Vatican II, 'become fully human'. For this vision to become a reality, we must rid ourselves of the temptation of the old form of clericalism. Clericalism is a scourge. It is about power, status, privilege. It has no place in the Christian way.

The priest is a man apart, but not any more apart than Jesus was among the women and men of His time. Faith lived with the people, community by community, bottom up, seems to be the focus for the future. Crises are not to be feared. It is through these crises that God grows closer to His people. It is in our weakness that we are strong. We are a Eucharistic community. Our weekly gatherings as such a community are now central for the nourishing and living out of our faith in the world.

Finally, these are not easy times for priests. We need to be assured that the message of the Cross is that God is found more easily in failure than in success. We are so fortunate to have the great encouragement and support of the people on the ground. We can now build on this.

APPENDIX THREE

GROUP '63 – THE STORY SO FAR …

The Group began when three priests, ordained together in Maynooth in 1963, met at the untimely funeral of a deceased classmate in September 1976. They felt that they should meet again, 'before the next funeral'. Each agreed to bring one other classmate of their own choice to a preliminary meeting in Salthill, Galway, and so, six priests attended the first meeting, on the 29 December, 1976. It is surely significant that thirty-seven years later, all six are still active members. The Group, which began with classmates, gradually became known to its members as *Group '63,* and the relationship to the class of '63 has been of significance ever since.

By the mid-seventies, radical changes were taking place in the lives of priests. The Latin-Mass Church, into which the group members had been ordained, had effectively ceased to exist. *Pange Lingua* had been replaced by *Michael Row the Boat Ashore,* altars faced the people and fellow-priests were leaving to get married. There was probably an unconscious need for priests to get together to try to make sense of what was happening.

Early meetings were relatively chaotic. If anybody had been asked, and they weren't, why did they gather, the answer would probably have been in the nature of – 'It's a good idea to meet.'

It eventually emerged that individual members had different visions of the attendance requirement. For most it was a very serious matter, for some, more of an optional affair. This difference of viewpoint eventually led to one member being effectively asked to leave, until such time as he was prepared to give his attendance a much greater priority. A second member left, because of the ongoing failure of the Group to afford enough weight to prayer and matters of importance. The membership was now down to four, but became five with the addition of a classmate who had returned to Ireland from ministry in the US. By any normal standard, anybody examining the 'progress' of the Group, would have reached the conclusion that it was doomed.

Indeed, how the Group survived for a number of years in these circumstances, remains a mystery. The turning point came during the summer of 1986. The two missing members had returned, but it was clear to everybody that the current structure, which itself is far too strong a word, simply couldn't or shouldn't continue. So the arrangements for each meeting were formalised, with a new starting time in the early afternoon, ending with an evening meal. A definite agenda was agreed. The gathering was to begin with Evening Prayer from the Breviary, followed by silent personal prayer – *Oratio Divina* – focusing on the following Sunday's Gospel. There was to be a rotating chairman, who would run two successive meetings and pre-circulate an agenda. It was seen as crucial that the temporary chairman should carry out his duties with great seriousness, keep members focused on what was happening, and run a tight ship.

Matters of a personal nature, which became known as 'personal time', were to be given a total priority. If a member or members had a significant personal situation, which merited lengthy discussion, that took priority over everything else, even to the extent of the set agenda being abandoned. This soon became, and has continued to be in the thirty-seven years that have passed since, the main cornerstone of the gathering. It has often been said that priests, possibly because they are all male, have a great flair for avoiding personal issues. The group became a safe environment where delicate discussions could take place in a supportive environment, and where peers could and would offer supportive comment, critical if needs be.

'Personal time' has always been distinguished from 'business time' – both appear on every agenda. The latter might refer to a new parish initiative, perhaps a book that some member thinks is worthy of attention from the others, or simply factual information of interest to priests. Following the conclusion of prayer at the beginning of the meeting, the chairman always asks each member whether they will require personal time or business time, and also to provide a rough estimate as to how much space should be allocated. On rare occasions, a member may say that he will be raising a serious personal issue, and it might need an hour or far more. Usually, discussion of a personal issue might take ten or twenty minutes or thereabouts, sometimes a lot less. However, the chairman will always ensure that each personal issue has been fully discussed, before moving on to the next item.

That the members come from different dioceses has probably been significant. For one thing, it means that insular diocesan matters are never discussed – nobody in Mayo is remotely interested in the trivial goings on in Waterford or Limerick. Confidentiality, which is seen as critical, is absolute, but perhaps easier, because of the diversity of distance. Meetings are arranged months ahead of time, and for the members, achieve a sacrosanct priority in their personal diaries. Occasionally, but extremely rarely, an outsider has been invited to attend a meeting and to talk to the group.

Attendance is compulsory, in the sense that if one priest simply can't attend, for example through illness, the meeting does not take place. It is either rearranged, or abandoned. This priority given to attendance is seen by all members as absolutely critical to the continuation of the enterprise. Meetings are held monthly, with a break in July, August and September. Having discovered the hard way that hotels are not well-suited to hosting afternoon gatherings, since 1992 meetings have been held in members' homes in the Shannon–Limerick region.

For a number of years, members have been taking a significant book – the last ones being *Faith Maps* by Michael Paul Gallagher and *Falling Upward* by Richard Rohr – and each member in turn prepares a summary of a chapter, and talks to a circulated printed paper on the subject. The other members would also have read the chapter, but at a less intense level than the main speaker, and a lively discussion usually ensues.

Voluntary groups, whose members have to drive cumulative totals of hundreds of miles, do not last for thirty-seven years, unless they are doing something right; unless they are fulfilling a need. So what do the members of *Group '63* get from each gathering, that is sufficient to explain its significant longevity? Whatever the answer is, words such as support and friendship, trust and confidentiality would be listed. 'Mission statements' would not be the normal stuff of *Group '63*, but if there were one, it might go something like this – This Group serves the needs of its members, by providing a safe and friendly environment, where issues of importance may be raised and dealt with in an atmosphere of trust and support, among peers and equals.

So everything in *Group '63* is perfect then? Far from it. There is a Russian proverb which says: No family can place a placard outside their home stating 'There is nothing wrong here.' In many ways, *Group '63* is a kind of family, and there have been disagreements and minor personal conflicts at different times, down through the years. The writer Flannery O'Connor described smugness as the great religious sin. After so many years together, there is a danger of the very kind of smugness that fails to challenge one another, a too-willing acceptance of 'this is how we are'. It is probably true that *every* group needs a bit more of 'this is how we could be'. The very support and friendship that has been a cornerstone of the group, can also become a formidable barrier to challenge and advancement.

Two final points: each member, if asked whether they look forward to the meetings, would answer a definite *Yes*. Indeed, if they didn't, why would they still be coming? Many years ago, a member left the country to work permanently in the US. He remains in the Group, intimately in touch with the other members and they with him. At the start of each meeting, he phones and each member in turn talks to him for as long as it takes, before the rest of the meeting proceeds. Members are also in regular contact with him outside the meetings.

For good or ill, it appears that membership of *Group '63* has many of the aspects of a life sentence!

Following the method of their formation.

Different methods for different ways of life

whatever that marks.

Epilogue

There is a lot of water under the proverbial bridge since I began writing this book. Heracletus said that you can't enter the same river twice. The water is constantly flowing, constantly changing. Writing this book has brought me down the road of remembering the significant people, events, and conversations that have shaped my life. But it does not stop there. Life continues to unfold. The God of Surprises is still at work.

And what a surprise Pope Francis has been! In the six months since becoming Pope he has been bringing us back to the message of Christ. What he is saying is very simple. He is bringing us to a clear understanding of what the Church is for, with emphasis on a humble Church, which looks out for the poor and brings them hope. He has strong words to say about authoritarianism, clericalism and the abuse of power.

Pope Francis has clearly indicated a need for a different vision of Church and he is spelling out by word and deed the importance of the common touch and a different kind of leadership. He said 'only within the concrete circumstances of daily life can one share in the faith and joy of the presence of Christ'. Could he be the one who has been sent to bring us all, in civil and religious worlds, back to putting the people, not institutions, at the centre? Is it possible that Francis could be the one to change history?

I have found myself very moved by the vision of Church he is setting out. It resonates deeply with me. The title of this book *Swimming Upstream* reflects something of my struggle with the kind of Church we had become, a church which I felt was too introverted, too clerical, too focused on itself. This kind of Church went against the grain of everything I believe about who we are called to be as a Christian people. I have found Francis inspiring, uplifting and encouraging. His words touch me profoundly. They affirm something of my own vision and encourage me, and the parish of Sixmile-bridge and Kilmurry, in the very imperfect ways we have been trying to forge new ways. His words also challenge us to go much further.

Of course Francis is only coming back to the central message of Vatican II. This council marked a huge shift. It opened the windows of the Church to greater interaction with and influence on the secular world. I and many of my generation, were energised by the whole thrust of Vatican II. We tried to work out how it should be applied on the ground. But gradually the Church turned inward again, perhaps fearful that real engagement might call it to change. Francis seems to be calling us back to Vatican II. He constantly critiques a Church that is 'wrapped up in its own world' as he likes to say, and calls us to be a Church which reaches out to people, especially those who are disadvantaged in any way. Watching Francis on television as he interacts with people in the places he visits in the City of Rome or at the World Youth Day in Rio, one cannot but notice how he loves to be among people. His personal warmth and his interest in them is very evident. By his words and actions, Francis is modelling a Church which loves humanity. 'For God so loved the world that he gave his only Son.' This gospel sentence is one I have always loved.

Even as Archbishop, Francis wanted to make the Church visible outside its buildings. He insisted that the Church must go to the people and not expect the people to come to the Church. His vision encourages us to keep developing this concept in Sixmilebridge and Kilmurry with our open-air Masses and 'area gatherings'. His vision helps us to see that the Masses we have celebrated on the side of hill, beside a lake, in a housing estate, in a cattle mart, at the railway station, at the crossroads and in a hurling field are a visible expression of the Church opening to the world outside the building. He challenges us to be present as often as we can at events with people as they move around doing their shopping, or work, but above all in their suffering. Francis has recently described the Church as a 'field hospital' for humanity. My own experience of the 'field hospital' is that it is often a place where you feel helpless, where there is nothing you can do but be present and 'journey with'. Few words are needed where physical and spiritual pain is borne from within … where no one can enter.

Part of what I have been trying to describe in this book is my attempt to discern and understand what is happening in society, in the world around me. I don't remember which theologian said that we must read the gospel with the bible in one hand and the newspaper in the other. I would add a third category here. We must read the gospel in the lives of ordinary people. Sometimes it isn't easy to understand what is going on around us but we must make an effort.

Again I go back to Francis. Recently I was reading about his early years. When he was thirteen, his father told him it was time for him to start work, whilst still continuing with his studies. He was shocked. The father arranged for him to work in a hosiery factory from 2 p.m. to 8 p.m. The school hours were from 8 a.m. to 1 p.m. He also worked as a cleaner, and did clerical work. He later said:

> The work I did was one of the best things I've done in my life … unemployed people are made to feel like they don't really exist. Dignity is not conferred by one's ancestry, family life or education. Dignity comes solely from work. It's very important that governments cultivate a culture of work.

The fact is we now live in a society where large-scale unemployment is seriously damaging lives – individuals, families and communities. It is resulting in a form of emigration that is draining the country of a bright young generation which could have major repercussions for this country. For example, an experienced medical doctor said to me recently that in a short time our hospitals will be relying on third-rate surgeons and consultants. The bright ones will have gone and won't come back.

The implications of the collapse of institutions too are enormous, leaving a deep legacy of confusion and distrust. We just had a referendum about whether the Seanad should be abolished or not. The low turnout (39%) clearly indicates that the political system has lost touch with the people. The ballot paper itself caused extraordinary confusion – another indication that people responsible for putting this together live in a bubble. This also illustrates that the systems that brought us to where we are now are obviously seriously flawed and in need of radical reform. But again to repeat what the book is saying – more of the same will not bring about recovery in the economy or in our institutions or in the renewal in the Church.

A Final Surprise

These last weeks a final surprise, which we cannot but record here, filled us with deep emotion and pride when Clare, after sixteen years in the wilderness, were crowned senior All-Ireland hurling champions after a replay. They won it with style and great skill. Two weeks earlier they won the under-21 final. A big number of the under-21 team are on the senior panel – five on the team proper, including a nineteen-year-old who scored three goals and three points in the senior final. A heading on the paper the following day read 'Breathtaking Final Will Go Down in History'.

Years ago, Raymond Smith wrote a book about hurling called *Clash of the Ash*. In it he said, 'Hurling brings out all the soul and passion of our race and does something for the really appreciative ones which can never be explained on paper.' It touches something deep in us in Clare, something about identity and belonging and pride in local place. We saw that as the team made the journey home on Sunday night with the Liam McCarthy Cup. Thousands gathered to welcome the team across the villages and some of the hurling heartlands of Clare, including Sixmilebridge. The gathering in Ennis was special. Thirty thousand from across the county, full of delight and pride in what our young team had done. A day (and a night) we will not easily forget.

Davy Fitzgerald managed this team. He is the first Clare man to win two senior All-Ireland hurling medals himself and manage another All-Ireland winning team. With the average age of this team at twenty-two there could be a lot more to come – only time will tell!

The replay was played on a Saturday. My homily at Mass in Sixmilebridge the following morning began by saying it would not be directly connected to the gospel story but it would be about what was very real for us in Sixmilebridge and Kilmurry and in Clare. I pointed out that Jesus proclaimed the message through stories and by connecting to real life. I congratulated the team and all involved. I focused on how they had prepared. At a time when role models and leaders are needed in all walks of life, in Clare and all across the country, we have new heroes and they are our own. What they have achieved is special – but how they prepared is an example for all young people. They brought a discipline to their ordinary lives, which was quite extraordinary. For example, at a time when substance and drink abuse is creating havoc in people's personal lives and in family life, these lads created an alcohol-free culture for themselves. In fact they have continued with that, not altogether but for the most part, since the final. After the match, Davy said 'they showed incredible resilience when Cork drew level with them in the fifty-third minute. That came from incredible inner strength and from the many sacrifices they have made to win this All-Ireland. They are such an honest bunch of lads, they never give up.' They are a young bunch of lads who obviously have a mission. They set high standards for themselves – mentally, physically and in developing their skills. They are also people who are close to one another, who have huge respect for one another, and for Davy – as he respects them.

One of the lovely things about them is the time they give to people who are less well off – the sick, the elderly and lonely and those who are disabled. There is no doubt in my mind that they will cope well with triumph. They are very definite role models for young people and they now have a mission as they visit parishes and schools around the county. They want not just to bring around the Liam McCarthy Cup but to engage young people especially in conversation about their lives and about taking leadership in the way they live today. This could transform a lot of other young people and made a huge contribution to communities around the county.

If I were to single out one thing about this win I would put it down to the leadership Davy has shown. One aspect of that is the extraordinary work he does on himself. By that I mean he works on his own inner world, and ensures he leads from a good place within himself. This is demanding work which requires discipline. There is a message here for all of us and especially those who are in leadership positions – obviously parents but also doctors, teachers, public servants, administrators, clergy, entrepreneurs, people in all walks of life – we cannot change anything if we don't change ourselves first. Unless we are looking after our own demons, our own inner struggles, our own contradictions, we will visit them on those we claim to serve. I personally find this a constant challenge but for me this inner work is vital.

I promised I would write this book only if there was a purpose in it. Is it possible that Church and State systems could learn from what is happening at local community level? Based on this idea is it time to articulate a vision or to reimagine an Ireland which can turn to the people – their talents and resources – for renewal and recovery? Could this be a topic worth considering? The *conversation* along these lines has already begun.

Local Churches have begun, albeit very slowly and indeed reluctantly, to move in this direction. Fortunately these have found a leader in Pope Francis. A radical change of attitude will be needed on the part of many Church leaders down the line. The road ahead will be long and difficult but at least it is encouraging to be moving in the right direction rather than to be continuing with a system that is clearly not working.

Maybe the time has come for others in leadership positions to recognise that the systems – political, banking, education, corporations and health are not working as they should be in the people's interest. A different kind of leadership is needed – a leadership that will empower people to take responsibility. Could Francis be the one who might change the course of history? Practically this will mean a radical change of direction within the systems.

In a sense the message was well articulated by Diarmaid Ferriter in the *Irish Times* of Saturday, 26 October 2013 when quoting another historian Gearóid O'Tuathaigh:

> What is striking is the almost total absence of any clearly articulated … social vision by political leaders in recent decades … The general statements of social policy have rarely ventured too far from the safe zone of economic managerialism which has become the general zone of political discourse. The failure to articulate, still less to systematically take steps to achieving … a persuasive vision of social solidarity, based on a set of values and principles that would enjoy wide public endorsement has resulted in a series of … statements … which continue to cause widespread frustration, confusion, disappointment and anger among different sections of the community.

This book is simply making the point – the people in their communities are moving forward. They now need the systems to follow.

A Born Leader

My interest in Clare hurling began with great days in Thurles in the 1970s when Fr Harry's team was meeting and beating the best, bar one. They were probably the unluckiest of all Clare teams not to win an All-Ireland. They won two National Leagues (the first national titles for decades) beating Kilkenny on both occasions. They were unlucky to meet a very strong Cork team in two Munster finals; Cork went on to win three All-Irelands in a row.

I regard Harry as a close friend and one who has provided me with great support in different ways over the years. He has given extraordinary leadership in extending himself to people in every walk of life whether they are churchgoers or not. He is a born leader and recognised as that. People have total respect for him. He's an absolute inspiration to me.

Davy Fitzgerald